Nature through
Science and Art

Nature through Science and Art

Susie Gwen Criswell

Foreword by Judith Gradwohl
Director, Office of Environmental Awareness, Smithsonian Institution

TAB Books
Division of McGraw-Hill, Inc.
Blue Ridge Summit, PA 17294-0850

FIRST EDITION
FIRST PRINTING

© 1994 by **Susie Gwen Criswell**.
Published by TAB Books.
TAB Books is a division of McGraw-Hill, Inc.
First edition © 1986 *Nature with Art: Classroom and Outdoor Art Activities with Natural History*
by Prentice Hall Press.

Library of Congress Cataloging-in-Publication Data
Criswell, Susie Gwen.
    Nature through science and art / Susie Gwen Criswell : foreword by
Judith Gradwohl.
        p.   cm.
    Includes bibliographical references (p.147) and index.
    ISBN 0-07-013783-8 (p)   ISBN 0-07-013782-X (h)
    1. Nature study—Activity programs. 2. Natural history—Study and
teaching—Activity programs. 3. Natural history illustration-
-Technique. 4. Art and science. I. Title.
QH54.5.C74 1993   93-38579
508—dc20   CIP

Acquisitions editor: Kimberly Tabor
Editorial team: Joanne Slike, Executive Editor
                Susan Wahlman Kagey, Managing Editor
                J. Bottomley, Editor
                Joann Woy, Indexer
Production team: Katherine G. Brown, Director
                Jan Fisher, Layout
                Ollie Harmon, Typesetting
                Cindi Bell, Proofreading
Design team: Jaclyn J. Boone, Designer
                Brian Allison, Associate Designer   HT1
Cover design and illustration: Craig Reese, Hanover, Pa.   4509

To John and Robinson

Acknowledgments

I would like to thank Kim Tabor, my editor at TAB Books, for her assistance in this project. The first edition was written in Foresta, within Yosemite National Park. I had the privilege of working with the fine staff of the Yosemite Institute during that time, and it is to these people I want to extend grateful recognition. Individuals I wish to thank are Vince Kehoe, Kathleen O'Connell, Elizabeth Hardie, Maggie Rivers, Mary Beth Hennessy, Bar Turner, Bob Pavlik, Lisa Fox, Pete McGee, Larry Prussin, and Pat O'Donnell for their support and assistance. Bobbie Criswell and Pat Perry gave the initial project invaluable assistance.

The second edition was written in Ithaca, New York, my current home. I would like to thank the people who have assisted me with their resources and time during the revision. Individuals that I would like to thank include John Schelhas, Kathleen O'Connell (again), Lynne Wilks and the rest of the writer's group, Cindy Kramer, John Hallas, and the Greenpath kids.

For permission to reprint the illustrations on pages xx, 8, 19, 21, 25, 33, 55, 112, 127, 129, and 137, grateful acknowledgment is extended to Shauna Ellett.

For permission to reprint the illustrations on pages 36, 99, 104, and 121, grateful acknowledgment is extended to Erika Perloff.

For permission to reprint the illustrations on pages 3, 11, 57, and 77, grateful acknowledgment is extended to Kathy Darrow.

For permission to reprint the photographs on pages 61, 86, and 93, grateful acknowledgment is extended to Roger McGeehee.

For permission to reprint the illustrations on pages 67 and 114, grateful acknowledgment is extended to Jenna Hallas.

CONTENTS

Foreword   xi

Introduction   xiii

1 Earth's elements   1
   1. Where does light originate?   2
   2. Why do we see color?   4
   3. What are warm & cool colors?   6
   4. What can be seen during the night?   7
   5. What are some cycles in nature?   10
   6. How does the earth's surface change?   12
   7. What is the makeup of soils?   15
   8. Why are sands different colors?   17
   9. Why do rocks have so many shapes & textures?   20
   10. What is in a fossil?   22
   11. Does nature use glue?   24
   12. Why do we have wind?   26
   13. Where do hurricanes & tornadoes come from?   28
   14. Where does snow come from?   30
   15. What is fire ecology?   32

2 Plant investigations   35
   1. What is photosynthesis?   36
   2. Are mushrooms plants?   38
   3. What are lichens?   40
   4. What are mosses?   42
   5. Why are some seeds & fruits fuzzy, sticky, or
      delicious?   45
   6. How does a seed become a plant?   46
   7. Why do plants have flowers?   49
   8. What are weeds?   51
   9. Why do plants & trees have leaves?   54
   10. How do coniferous & deciduous trees differ?   56
   11. What is leaf litter?   58
   12. Why do trees have bark?   61
   13. What is forest succession?   63
   14. How do trees benefit wildlife?   65
   15. How do plants help people?   68
   16. Why should we care about tropical rain forests?   70

3 Animal explorations 75

1. What are the smallest animals? 76
2. What do bees & butterflies eat? 79
3. What are mollusks? 81
4. Do earthworms eat soil? 83
5. How do spiders make a web? 85
6. Where do frogs go during the winter? 88
7. How do feathers help birds? 90
8. Why do animals have whiskers? 93
9. Why do some animals have
   hooves & some have paws? 96
10. Why do animals have differently shaped teeth? 98
11. Do all animals respond to either light or sound? 101
12. Why are some animals camouflaged? 103
13. Can some animals change their disguises? 106
14. What kinds of shelters do animals build? 108
15. Do animals have a memory? 110
16. How smart are animals? 113

4 Human dimensions 115

1. Why is the human hand so miraculous? 116
2. How important is our sense of smell? 118
3. How do our ears work? 120
4. Why did early people draw murals? 123
5. What were some of the first tools? 125
6. What did early Native Americans
   use for sewing & weaving? 127
7. Why do people tell stories? 130
8. Why did John Muir keep a sketchbook/journal? 132
9. Why do people write about nature? 134
10. Why is hazardous waste a human concept? 136
11. How can photography help to communicate about
    nature? 138
12. Why do some places capture our attention? 141
13. What makes a human community? 143

Additional reading 147

Index 153

If facts are the seeds that later produce knowledge and wisdom, then the emotions and the impressions of the senses are the fertile soil in which the seeds must grow.

Rachel Carson
The Sense of Wonder

OUR CHILDREN face a very different world from the one we were born into. Environmental considerations that are important now might well become critical over the next few decades. Today's children need to know and appreciate the natural world if they want to leave a cleaner and healthier planet than the one they inherited.

From breathtaking glacial ravines of Yosemite Valley to weeds growing in neglected rain gutters, *Nature through Science and Art* encourages young people to learn more about the natural world. Combining careful observation with artistic rendering, scientific inquiry, and a sense of adventure, this book will both entertain and inspire. The activities will be valuable for all children, even those who do not have a strong scientific or artistic bent.

The particular beauty in Susie Criswell's approach is that the activities foster a greater understanding and appreciation of any piece of the natural world. Any backyard or city park can provide material for scientific observation and artistic endeavor. This focus on local nature is just as important as awareness of international environmental issues like tropical forest conservation and the protection of coral reefs. The exposure to local environmental conditions through activities in this book will help children understand the value of healthy ecosystems, whether in a local natural area or the Amazon basin.

Although the activities in this book are intended for children in the upper primary grades, I think that people of all ages could benefit from taking a break to look closely at the nature around us. Perhaps the most important lesson in *Nature through Science and Art* is that we all have a bit of scientist and artist in us, and we can use these skills to appreciate the play of light on spring leaves, how animals move, and all of the details in nature that we usually overlook.

Judith Gradwohl, Director
Office of Environmental Awareness
Smithsonian Institution

xi

I REMEMBER an afternoon in early September, when a dozen fifth graders and I were perched on a pile of granite boulders. Our arms were outstretched while our view took in the glacial-carved Yosemite Valley; we were soaring hawks. After descending from our "flight," the various members of the group settled in to draw what we had imagined. We had previously discussed how hawks' eyes are like telescopes, able to spot their prey at two to three times the distance that a human could see. We had also talked about how a hawk, with a single glance, can take in a scene that a person would be able to view only by laboriously scanning a whole landscape piece by piece. Soon, the drawings included both the tops of the trees and mice scurrying in the shadows below. The meandering river and snakes slithering among the grasses were also drawn as the children imagined vision through a hawk's eyes. The children were combining science and art to view nature.

For many years, I walked in the woods with children daily. As an instructor for the Yosemite Institute, I encouraged my students to come closer to nature to learn what it had to teach them. Since leaving the granite walls and thousand foot waterfalls of my Yosemite classroom, I continue to teach, write, and illustrate in the field of environmental education.

I regularly talk with teachers, group leaders, and parents. The main point I stress to them, and to you, is to take walks with your children and approach nature with open eyes and a willingness to explore. Then return to an indoor workspace, or better yet, remain outdoors and, through drawing and discussing things you noticed, become better acquainted with the world you inhabit.

Many elementary-school students can describe how tropical rain forests are being destroyed and how whales, rhinos, and elephants are being threatened to extinction. Posters, T-shirts, and bumper stickers proclaim our children's environmental awareness. Yet I've found that when we ask children about the need for protecting the soil, wildlife, and watersheds that are a part of their city or home town, they know much less. While it is important to be aware of global environmental problems, one can better understand and preserve wildlife and habitat on a

local level. It is a pleasurable experience to walk the land, swim in the stream, or watch the birds that you have come to know and protect. Young people will understand and grow to love their surroundings when they are encouraged to explore, draw, and become aware of the wildlife and region where they live.

Science & art transport nature's secrets

Years ago, John Muir said, "Let nature be your teacher." Nature's lessons expand and overlap the boundaries of traditional classroom learning. This overlap is important, as most children learn best when offered a variety of learning experiences, illustrating a single topic from several directions. By combining science and art, more children can grasp an understanding of nature's principles.

For example, when children take water samples from a pond, study them under a microscope, and later make abstract drawings from sketches they drew of the protozoa, they are combining science with art to study nature. Observation is a key element in both science and art. One of the best ways to teach children to look closely is to encourage art at home and in the classroom. As children get better at drawing what they see, they become better at observing the world around them.

Although many people see science and art as very different, with science being factual and art being intuitive, I find many similarities. Science and art are both processes of inquiry, or ways of gaining knowledge about the world. They are both processes that start with ideas that have to be developed. Both science and art require that a child take risks, and both allow for creative freedom and mistakes. Children respond well to the blending of the two and have fun in the process.

Book description

While living in Yosemite I wrote a book called *Nature with Art*, combining my art training with many of the ideas generated during my years as a field instructor. *Nature through Science and Art* has evolved from the skeleton of that book. This edition offers a large array of art activities and also adds scientific research questions to trigger both the left and the right sides of the brain.

The activities in *Nature through Science and Art* are designed for children in the upper primary grades. The 60 natural history questions are divided into four chapters based on physical science, botany, zoology, and human ecology. Each natural history question is posed with science research questions and art activities to help illustrate it.

The research questions and art activities in this book can be molded to meet your children's level of interest. Check the table of contents, mark the pages that sound interesting to you, and use this book as you would a handy reference. This book should not sit on a shelf collecting dust; it should be taken into the field, pulled out of a backpack regularly, and become worn from use.

The research questions represent a range of difficulty levels. Some can be answered in the field; others might need to be researched in the library. Teaching the learning process can be more important than teaching the answers, so don't feel you must have all the answers before you go out with the children.

This book is intended for the adult leader. If you have spent a great deal of time in nature, you probably already know what to avoid and what to take with you. Packing a first-aid kit and bug repellent will make your excursions safer and more pleasant. Teach the children caution around the streams, embankments, and small cliff edges you might encounter in your walks. You should take certain other common-sense precautions, such as teaching the children to recognize any poisonous plants or animals.

Many of you are teachers, group leaders, and parents who are interested in taking children outdoors. The idea of going outdoors armed with natural history information and science research questions offers you ideas and inspiration. But the part about the art activities might scare you just a little. After all, you might not have drawn anything yourself in many years, and the thought of having to instruct others in art activities might seem more than challenging. But relax! You can do it.

Don't worry if you are not artistic!

You do not have to be an art teacher to use this book. As a matter of fact, setting up an atmosphere in which you tell the children that you are going to draw along with them, even if you have not drawn in years, often results in a pleasant give-and-take spirit where the children feel comfortable offering you tips and suggestions. Drawing with the children shows them you are interested in exploring nature with them. It is okay if you do not know the names of all the birds, trees, and rocks you draw. As the teacher, parent, or group leader taking part in an art activity, you are offering an opportunity for the children to spend time outdoors taking note of and exploring many of the little things in nature that often go unnoticed.

Some drawing tips

You can share these art and drawing tips with the children whether you are working indoors or outside.

1. To see better, don't draw into a direct light. If you can, put the subject to the side or move so that the light source or sun is behind you.

2. Sit quietly for a while to let yourself be drawn into the moment. Don't rush; take your time to let nature resume what it was doing before you arrived.

3. Draw the obvious shapes or objects of interest; don't let yourself get bogged down or confused by starting with the details.

4. In drawing perspective, things at a distance seem smaller, narrower, higher, and simpler than things close up. Putting one thing in front of another helps to offer perspective. It is fun to try to get unusual perspectives—for example, drawing from the base of a tree looking up.

5. Encourage the children to break away from stereotypes. For example, don't draw a puffy cotton ball for a cloud. Really look at the cloud to see its shape.

Materials & supplies

Each art activity has a section where the specific drawing materials needed are listed, but the majority require only a sketchbook/journal and pencils or pens. A drawing board is also mentioned; a drawing board could be any hard surface

that allows you to draw outside on paper; for example, a clipboard, a small chalkboard, or a lapboard.

The following supply list is meant for you and each accompanying child for any outdoor excursion. The children should be encouraged to bring their own equipment. The list starts with the most essential items and follows with others that are handy to include:

Essential:

1. Clothes and shoes that are appropriate for the weather.
2. A lightweight book bag or backpack to carry both your materials and objects found along the way.
3. A sketchbook/journal (*more on this at the end of the list).
4. Pens and pencils for taking notes and drawing. Always bring extra.
5. Snacks and water.
6. Hat, sunglasses, and sunscreen.

Handy:

7. Two small jars for collecting. Bring one with holes in the top for live specimens and another without holes for sand, snow, or other collectibles.
8. Two plastic bags for larger collectibles that might be wet or damp.
9. Field guides to birds, animal tracks, and insects.
10. Hand lens or magnifying glass.

*A sketchbook/journal is a great tool for recording drawings, jotting down clues for science investigations, and staying organized. With a sketchbook/journal, children can record not only what they see, but also what they are thinking. They should be encouraged to write and draw in it at any time while "in the field," at home, at school, or while waiting for a bus. Look at pages 133–134 in chapter 4, "Human dimensions," for instructions on how to construct a sketchbook/journal.

Who has the time?

As busy teachers, parents, camp counselors, nature center staff members, and others, you probably are wondering when you would have time to take a group of young people into nature. First of all, you needn't go far. Your field journey might begin the moment you walk out the door. A line of ants marching down a cracked sidewalk, a building cumulus cloud that covers the sky, or the twining ivy growing up a tree—all might be explored without having to leave the front yard.

Other ideas for finding time include:

1. If you work with another adult in a classroom situation, one of you can take a small group of youngsters for 20 minutes a day outside to do an activity on the playground.

2. Consider holding a science or art class outside once a week.

3. Combine time blocks with other educators and make a longer period of time available to work with children outside.

4. Introduce the activity at school or at camp, and have the children develop it on their own time and share it with others later.

5. Put together a list of ideas from this book for parents, camp counselors, or babysitters to do over the summer.

Trips into the field require more time and effort, but a well-planned visit to garden areas, vacant lots, local parks, and waterfront areas can promote long-lasting results. Other public areas of interest to explore nature through science and art could be a zoo, an aquarium, botanical gardens, or a natural history museum close to your home or school. Perhaps you will be less distracted by familiar surroundings and more drawn into nature if you can get out of town to your local nature center, a friendly farm, or any publicly owned lands. I encourage you to try to visit protected wild areas with your children. If you are near the ocean, walk down a beach and assemble your group away from the popular recreation areas; if you are near a protected forest, hike a couple miles up the trail away from any parking lots. The peace that you find away from the crowds can help inspire the discoveries to be made in nature.

Developing a nature area close to your home or school can provide the children with a close-up view and personal knowledge of the plants, insects, and birds that become regular visitors. A close-to-home nature area also eases access for those who are disabled or unable to take trips into the field very often. Have the children help plan the nature area, plant flowers, and maintain a bird feeder or bird bath to promote a sense of responsibility and a source of pride.

Many of you might have a limited area to work with, such as a corner of the school yard or a fire escape on your apartment building. The size of the area does not really matter. Keep in mind that weeds growing in neglected rain gutters carry out complete life cycles by attracting insects and other pollinators. Within your nature area, you can grow plants, attract animals, and build a sense of beauty and life in areas that might now appear lifeless.

Consider first the amount of sunlight your nature area receives and your climate. These two factors should influence what plants you cultivate. Ask your local nursery for advice on native plants for your area. Some tips on what some favorite pollinators prefer:

- **Hummingbirds:** scarlet petunias, scarlet impatiens, fuchsias, nasturtiums, trumpet vines, scarlet sage, and larkspur.

- **Bees:** apples, pears, snapdragons, strawberries, pennyroyal mint, clover, cherries, and borage.

- **Butterflies:** zinnias, marigolds, thistles, mint, pinks, nasturtiums, and larkspur.

- **Moths:** honeysuckle, phlox, and gardenias.

Once the plants and insects are thriving, more birds and—depending on the size of your area—other animals will appear. Trees should be planted in a yard or in large barrels. Put a bird bath on some bricks or rocks in the nature area. Containers of flowers to attract insects and birds should be placed four to five feet from the bird bath, in order to avoid providing cover for bird-hunting cats. This area will inspire the children to want to spend time outside taking care of the little world they have helped to create.

Whether you create your own nature area or take your children to other destinations, the science and art ideas inspired by spending time outdoors with children in nature are limitless. The 60 nature questions are examples of the multitude that children will ask. I hope the science and art ideas will inspire you and the children to continue investigating the natural world. Take your children and look under rocks, climb trees, examine the parts of a flower, and get your feet wet in creeks. These lessons are the most memorable and can inspire a life-long love of the natural world.

A natural enthusiasm for learning occurs when children are encouraged to explore nature.

Earth's elements

EVEN THOUGH I have been studying and teaching about nature for years, I still consider the forces that allow life to exist on earth as unfolding mysteries. How interrelated are sunlight, soil, water, and our atmosphere in sustaining life on the planet? How does a changing climate affect ecosystems on earth? How would the erosion of a riverbank influence a coral reef a hundred miles away? Scientists are investigating these and many other questions about earth's elements in both local and global studies.

Your children's sense of creativity can be enhanced by introducing them to the many mysteries and objects of beauty to be found in nature. A handful of sand can be examined for its diverse colors and weight, snow can be molded and melted to reveal its properties, and a hurricane's wind force can be imagined and drawn. You and your children can discuss the earth's elements while observing a flooded stream bank or watching an oak log burning in the night. Remind the children how all life is dependent on the elements of nature. Experiment with sunshine, soil, and snow. These elements have been with us most of our lives, yet we rarely take the time to observe and understand them.

The research questions and activities in this chapter offer you a framework in which to introduce the elements of the earth. Learning about light in "Light of day drawing" demonstrates how the sun's power and light changes throughout the day. The children learn to associate the color they are seeing with the sun's rays. It becomes clear that without the sun, we would have no light, heat, or life as we know it. "Cycle drawing" helps illustrate the concept of the water cycle and many other cycles found in nature. Sand and soil are explored in "Sand painting" and "Clay impressions." The study of fire takes place while the children work on "Charcoal drawings." These and other activities in this chapter help youngsters observe closely and better understand the forces found in the sun, rain, soil, and atmosphere of our planet.

1. Where does light originate?

In our solar system, heat and light come from the sun, a star 93 million miles away from the earth. Like all stars, the sun is a great ball of hot gases that pours out a huge amount of heat and light and other energy. Only a tiny part of that energy reaches us. But the energy we receive is enough to light and heat the earth. The light we see takes 8 minutes to travel from the sun to the earth.

Our sun is a medium-sized star among billions of other stars in our galaxy, the Milky Way. The Milky Way is only one of millions of galaxies. Our sun is the closest star to the earth. The sun is 108 times larger than the earth. Simply put, the sun is a giant thermonuclear reactor burning hydrogen into helium. Light is the waste product put off as the hydrogen is made into helium. Our sun, believed to be about 10 billion years old, is only in the middle of its life.

The moonlight that we see is really the sun's light reflecting off the moon's surface. Besides sunlight, other natural sources of light reside in phosphorescent fireflies, a variety of fungi, and bioluminescent animals that glow in the ocean.

Research questions

Information to read aloud and research with your children:

Everything that we see either reflects light or gives off light. Can you feel the heat of the sun instantly when it is a sunny day and part of your body is shaded and another part is exposed to the sun? Is the sun-exposed part of your body more lit up? How have scientists been able to capture the sun's light and heat and use it to form energy? Do you feel differently during a sunny day than you do during an overcast day? Why?

Light of day drawing

Outdoor activity
Time needed: 15 minutes during sunrise, noon, and sunset
Materials needed:

- ❑ Alarm clock
- ❑ Sketchbook/journal or drawing paper
- ❑ Black, white, and gray chalk or pastels
- ❑ Drawing boards
- ❑ Outdoor thermometer

1. Find out what time the sun will be rising for the morning you want to conduct the activity. Set the alarm clock for half an hour before sunrise to get your children awake and ready to draw the sunrise and the light it presents.

2. Go to a nearby spot with trees or boulders at sunrise with the art supplies. First have the children record the air temperature. Also have them place their hands on the boulders and tree trunks. Have the group concentrate on drawing the visible light and shadows. Observe and draw a large boulder or a tree trunk. Note and draw the lit-up parts of the object and the shadowed parts.

3. Return to the same spot two more times throughout the day, once around noon and again at sunset. Each time have the children record the temperature and place their hands against the solid object to note any changes. Redraw the same tree or boulder, including the different shadows. Observe where the sun is located and note how it causes this change of temperature and shadows.

4. Each person should make a total of three different drawings, noticing the light source during each drawing. Compare the early morning temperatures and shadows with the midday and sunset temperatures and shadows.

The day's shadows and colors vary as the sunlight changes.

2. Why do we see color?

Light is called white when all of the light waves that travel from the sun are combined. Sunlight is a combination of red, orange, yellow, green, blue, and violet light. Separating white light into the color band of the spectrum is possible because all light travels in waves, and each color has a different wavelength. A rainbow or a prism separates these light waves and displays the separate colors of sunlight. In a rainbow, the colors are spread out side by side in a beautiful arch. Red is always on the outside edge of a rainbow, with violet on the inside. Red has the longest waves and violet has the shortest, with the others graded in between.

The different colors we see during the morning, afternoon, and evening are the result of the different angles at which light waves intercept with the atmosphere. For example, when longer wavelengths predominate, at sunset, they act as a filter allowing only some colors to be visible, such as the reds of alpenglow. The reds and brilliant colors we see at sunrise and sunset are also the result of pollution or particles in the atmosphere. These particles also act as filters.

If, for example, a box painted red has a light shining on it, why does it appear red? The paint's pigment has the ability to reflect certain portions of white light and absorb others. Red pigment absorbs all the other color waves and sends back only the red waves, so the box looks red. This explanation is true for all the colors we see.

Chlorophyll reflects green light and absorbs the other colors of the leaves.

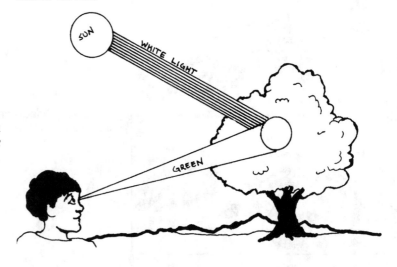

Different animals see different parts of the spectrum. For example, rattlesnakes have infrared receptors, using heat detection to "see" their world. Animals such as birds, lizards, frogs, fish, and even insects are able to see bright colors much the way we do. Horses, dogs, and cattle are colorblind; they cannot detect colors.

Research questions

Information to read aloud and research with your children:

Rainbows are only seen when the sun is behind the observer and falling water is in front. Rainbows can be formed from water from a storm cloud, a lawn sprinkler, or the mist above a waterfall. In all cases, water droplets form the waterfall. How do water droplets cause rainbows? Compare them to a prism. You can make a rainbow by using the fine mist of a garden hose. With your back to the sun when it is low in the sky, place your finger over the spray until it comes out at a wide angle. A rainbow will appear in the water. You can see it best against a dark background.

Indoor or outdoor activity
Time needed: 30 minutes
Materials needed:

Colors in nature
watercolor painting

- ❑ Watercolor paper or any thick drawing paper
- ❑ Box of watercolors
- ❑ Brushes
- ❑ Cup of water

1. After a discussion about how we see color, have the group prepare to work with watercolors. Place the water and paints carefully to avoid spills and to enable sharing.

2. Each child can paint a rainbow reflecting the colors of the spectrum in the natural order: red, orange, yellow, green, blue, and violet, with red on the top and violet on the bottom.

3. Experiment with painting other colorful objects found in nature. When using watercolors, light colors should be painted first and left to stand; darker colors can be added and painted over the lighter colors to make a mixed color. To

2. Why do we see color?   5

lighten a color, add more water to a color. For example, to make pink, you use red and add more water in your brush.

3. What are warm & cool colors?

Colors are separated into the blue/green "cool" and the red/yellow "warm" shades. White and the cooler shades reflect light, and black and the warmer shades absorb it. White clothing is cooler than black clothing on a hot sunny day, for light is also heat.

People not only see different colors, but they also interpret different messages from the colors. When you see a blue/green picture, it feels cool, and reds/yellows feel warm. This information is useful to not only scientists and artists, but all of us in understanding the use of color in communicating with people. For example, when looking at a snowy winter picture, viewers feel the cold of the white-blue-gray snow; they feel the warmth when yellow and red flames are included in a picture of a campfire scene.

Research questions

Information to read aloud and research with your children:

On a warm day, investigate how the sun's heat is absorbed by different colors. To do this, place pieces of construction paper of various colors in direct sunlight, being sure to include black and white. Place equal-sized ice cubes in clear plastic sandwich bags and seal the bags. Have one ice cube for every sheet of paper. Place the cube in the plastic bag in the center of each piece of paper and watch. Which cube begins to melt first? Which different colors absorb more heat and cause the ice to melt more rapidly? After about 15 minutes, see which bag has the most water in it. You can also lay thermometers on different pieces of colored paper in the sun outdoors and record the different temperatures after 15 minutes.

Warm and cool pictures

Indoor or outdoor activity
Time needed: 30 minutes
Materials needed:

- ❑ Sketchbook/journal or drawing paper
- ❑ Markers or crayons
- ❑ Drawing boards

1. Discuss warm and cool colors and talk about how warm colors absorb the sun's heat more readily than cool colors. Have each person do the following steps.

2. Divide up markers or crayons into the warm and cool colors. Warm colors are reds, oranges, and yellows. Cool colors are blues, grays, white. Purples and greens are a mix of both hot and cool colors.

3. Draw a picture using predominantly warm colors. Then make a picture using mostly blues, grays, white, and black. Have the children discuss how the pictures make them feel.

These girls are deciding if the colors of their markers are warm or cool colors.

Exploring nature at night is fascinating. By going outside with a flashlight, you will restore some color to objects. If the moon is out, turn your flashlight off, and let your eyes adjust. Familiar places have a different appearance at night, and distant objects might appear further away.

4. What can be seen during the night?

More animals are active during the night than during the day. Animals of the night are well prepared for limited light. Owls use their large eyes and bats use echolocation to determine their surroundings. Many animals, such as bears, use a keen sense of smell to get around. Fireflies attract their mates using their flashing lights. Many animals prefer the cloak of darkness to assist them in their hunting.

As you explore, keep an eye to the sky to see the stars and planets shine. Remember that the light of the moon and the planets is light reflected from the sun. While the stars do generate their own light, they are seen from such distances that it might have taken many, many years for their light to have reached earth.

Using a flashlight on a night walk enables you to observe nocturnal animals.

Research questions

Information to read aloud and research with your children:

Try to spend time observing the night sky completely away from a city's light source. What things reflect moonlight at night? For example, rivers, lakes, and new-fallen snow reflect

light. When you are away from the city, the light of the full moon illuminates your surroundings enough so that you can see shapes, but you can see little color. On the other hand, away from the city's lights on a moonless night, almost all color and vision disappear into the dark. Contrast the number of stars visible on a clear moonless night in a city with the amount of stars visible in the country.

Conduct an investigation on bioluminescent fireflies. How do fireflies make their light and why? Explore how bats use echolocation. How do city lights affect nocturnal wildlife?

Outside activity
Time needed: 15–30 minutes
Materials needed:

❑ Sketchbook/journal or drawing paper
❑ Crayons
❑ Drawing boards
❑ Blankets

Nighttime drawing

1. Sit on blankets in an open area at night. Listen to the night sounds. Once everyone's eyes have adjusted and all have settled down, prepare to begin drawing. Each person should do the following steps.

2. Make a drawing without using flashlights. This activity demonstrates how difficult it is to see color at night. Draw the trees or landscape surrounding the group, selecting whatever crayon feels the most appropriate.

3. Observe the drawings the next morning in the daylight. The children will enjoy seeing what colors they used and how their night picture appears in the light.

4. Another nighttime drawing activity is to draw a night sky, including the moon, on a piece of black construction paper, using gold and silver crayons or glitter paint. Repeat the moon drawing activity once a week for a month (on clear nights). The drawings help to illustrate the varying phases of the moon and varying visibility of the stars during the moon's different phases.

5. What are some cycles in nature?

Cycles are like circles in that they have no beginning and no end. Almost everything in nature is a part of a cycle and is always undergoing a change. For example, water has a cycle. It has three forms in this cycle: solid when it is ice or snow; liquid when it is water; gas when it is vapor or steam. Observe the most familiar form of water, as a liquid, in a backyard birdbath. The sun shines down on the birdbath causing the water to heat up and change to a gas in the process of evaporation. This vapor rises into the atmosphere to form clouds. If the temperature falls below freezing, the vapor freezes and forms snow. The snow falls down into the backyard birdbath. The sun comes out and melts the snow into a liquid. The cycle is complete. The water cycle depends on the sun or some other source of heat.

All forms of life operate in a cycle. Plants and animals begin life as tiny seeds. They are nurtured and fed and grow into young plants and animals. They begin to mature and develop methods to reproduce themselves. They are fertilized when the male and female are joined together. After fertilization, the new seed begins a life, and the old plant or animal dies and returns to the soil, enabling new growth to occur.

Cycles are everywhere in nature. Rocks break down, forming sand, and sand is pressurized together, forming new rocks. The air we breathe is exhaled as carbon dioxide; plants take in carbon dioxide and release oxygen: and we use oxygen to breathe. Once we understand this integrated approach to how the natural world works, we can better understand how we are linked to everything else on the planet.

Research questions

Information to read aloud and research with your children:

Living in the temperate zone, we have four seasons that go in a cycle. What are signs of the cycle of the seasons? How do the plants and animals survive the cycle of the seasons?

Think about and explain a cycle for the air you breathe, the water you drink, the food you eat, and the place you live. Can a cycle be interrupted or broken? What would an example of that situation be? Explain the life cycle for people.

Cycles are essential
components of
nature that help to
teach about renewal
and change.

Cycle drawing

Indoor or outdoor activity
Time needed: 15 minutes
Materials needed:

- ❑ Drawing paper
- ❑ Pencils
- ❑ Drawing boards

1. After you discuss cycles, have the children sit in a circle,
   prepared to draw. Mention that they will each be contributing

5. What are some cycles in nature?   11

to a story as the paper comes to them. Explain that the picture should somehow reflect a cycle within nature (water cycle, mineral cycle, oxygen cycle, life cycle, etc.).

2. Each child has one minute to begin their own drawing. They then pass the drawing to the next person. Let the children know they each have one minute to add their contribution to each drawing that comes to them as the drawings rotate around the circle.

3. Continue until each child's drawing goes around the entire circle.

4. After the drawings are finished, have each child interpret what their cycle drawing started out to be and how it changed.

6. How does the earth's surface change?

Our solid earth is not as solid as it appears. Even the rocks within mountains change. The weathering of mountains is constant, but usually these changes are on a very slow and grand scale. In contrast, earthquakes and their fault lines change the contours of the earth's surface with sudden movements. The aftermath of an earthquake often includes landslides, fires, and tidal waves that further reshape the earth's surface.

The core of the earth is believed to be between 4000°F and 8000°F. Here on the surface, we are hardly aware of the furnace below us. Through the forces of geysers, hot springs, and especially volcanoes, we are made conscious of the heat deep within the earth. Volcanic eruptions spread their outpourings of lava, gases, and ash onto the surface, creating different land forms.

Erosion and diastrophism are the processes that contribute to the formation of much of the earth's surface. *Weathering* and *erosion* are the wearing away of rocks and soils due to trampling, wind, rain, and snow. *Diastrophism* is the process by which the earth's crust is upturned, broken, slanted, and folded. Most of the forces of diastrophism are deep within the earth, hidden in the earth's plates and molten rock, while weathering and erosion work openly upon the surface.

The greatest force of erosion is moving water. Billions of gallons of water run off to the seas every year, pulling with them millions of tons of mud, clay, and mineral fragments. These moving minerals change the face of the earth, carving valleys, changing rivers, and depositing sandbars. The ocean does not erode the earth as much as swift streams, but along some vulnerable coastlines the ocean's waves crash onto the shore with a powerful force. The ocean can build up as well as break down. Where the shore is gently sloping with a shallow bottom, the waves deposit the sand on shore, forming sandbars. These sandbars can grow large enough to enclose a lagoon, creating a new habitat for living things.

Information to read aloud and research with your children:

Research questions

Have you felt earthquakes before? Earthquakes occur when plates of the earth's crust push under or against one another. These plates have been moving and adjusting throughout the history of the earth. Are further earthquakes inevitable? What can we do to help protect ourselves from the destruction brought on by earthquakes?

Have you ever witnessed a sandbar in its changing form along a shore of a lake or the ocean? Keep track of the shore of a nearby pond or stream bank. Do you notice where it is undergoing changes due to erosion? How do these changes affect the rest of the waterway? Are stream channels forever changing their course? Can you find evidence of these changes?

Creating a landscape

Indoor or outdoor activity
Time needed: 1 hour
Materials needed:

- ❏ Cardboard boxes
- ❏ Objects from nature such as rocks, sand, leaves, and sticks
- ❏ Paper
- ❏ Pencil
- ❏ Crayons, colored pencils, markers, or paint
- ❏ Scissors
- ❏ Large plastic bag or shallow bowl

1. Discuss the variety of surfaces that the earth has and how the earth is always undergoing changes. Small groups work well in this activity.

2. Each group should create a model of an interesting earth surface. Within a cardboard box, construct water bodies, mountains, valleys, volcanoes, sandbars, or islands. Use rocks, sand, leaves, ferns, and colors to replicate the features of the landscape. Water can be put in place by using a shallow bowl or lining the box with plastic and pouring water in part of the box.

3. Each group can present their earth surface construction to the rest of the children. Have them explain how the different earth surfaces go through inevitable changes.

When a group creates a model of a landscape, cooperation and discussion are necessary.

14   Earth's elements

The soil is a constantly changing part of the earth's crust that is a few inches deep in some places and hundreds of feet deep in others. Soils greatly influence how well plants grow, and the plants, in turn, affect the soil. Soils contain a mixture of ingredients, including sands, rocks, dead organic matter, plant roots, small animals, and microorganisms, plus air and water. The different combinations of a soil's makeup results in different nutrients and acidity. These factors influence plant growth.

If you were to dig a hole and could see a profile of the layers of soil, often you would see three different layers. The first is called topsoil. Topsoil contains a great deal of organic matter from the trees, plants, and animals that it supports. The second layer is often lighter in color than topsoil and contains more clay. The third layer is called the parent material of the soil. It is developed by the wearing away of rocks, which is the first step in forming soil. This layer is formed from volcanic, glacial, wind, or water activity, or from the changes brought on rocks by the earth's heat or pressure.

The second layer, which includes the clay particles, is especially interesting. Clay particles are very small, and they usually carry an electrical charge that helps bind them together, making clay extremely sticky and slippery to the touch. The minute particle size and general compactness means that little air or water can circulate in these soils. Clay is moldable when wet, yet it sticks together and remains coherent when dry. It is a material that has many uses worldwide.

Information to read aloud and research with your children:

Research questions

The three principle ways that soil textures are described are sandy, silty, or clay-like. The clay particles in soils are the smallest of the three. They are so small that even a powerful light microscope would not make them visible. Coarse-textured soils (sandy or silty) do not hold a large amount of water, while clay soils permit very little water to pass through them. How would you determine what the texture of your soil most resembles? Do you know if the soil in your area has much clay in it?

Preparing natural clay

Outdoor activity
Time needed: A couple of days
Materials needed:

- ❏ Natural clay bed
- ❏ Newspapers
- ❏ ¼-inch mesh sieve
- ❏ Coffee cans
- ❏ Hammer or pounding rocks
- ❏ Water
- ❏ Window screen wire
- ❏ Cloth-lined bowls
- ❏ Shovels

1. Inquire around your local area as to where a clay deposit would be available to you. For information, contact your local county cooperative extension agent or a pottery instructor at a local college. These people should know the clay conditions in your area. Have the children assist you with the following steps.

2. Select a clay deposit that is as free as possible from impurities—that is, sand, gravel, dirt, plant roots, and so forth. Dig enough clay to fill the coffee cans.

3. Spread the clay out on the newspaper and place it in the sun to dry completely.

4. The clay will dry in hard lumps. With the hammer or rocks, break up the lumps into a fine powder. Do not crush any rock into the clay; be sure to remove the rocks.

5. Sift the powder clay through the sieve and remove the pebbles.

6. Pour the sifted clay into the coffee can until the can is about two-thirds full. Cover the clay with water until it is completely saturated and covered to the top of the can.

7. Using your hands, stir the clay to evenly distribute the water throughout.

8. Allow the clay to soak for two hours or until the mixture is the consistency of thick cream.

9. Pour this cream mixture through a piece of window screen into another coffee can.

10. Let this strained mixture sit overnight or until the clay has settled to the bottom. Pour off the clear liquid on top. Try not to stir up the thick "slip" underneath.

11. Pour the remaining thick slip into the cloth-lined bowls. As the cloth absorbs the water, the slip stiffens and separates from the cloth. The clay is then ready to store in covered cans. Clay improves with age, if stored properly. It should be stored wetter than needed to work with, because the clay will dry out when taken out of cans to be used and wedged.

12. Wedge the clay before using it. *Wedging* is the thorough kneading, pounding, and repeated slicing of the clay to get rid of air bubbles inside it.

Clay prepared by children involves the work of many hands.

Sand is loose, granular particles of worn or broken-down rock, finer than gravel and coarser than dust. Sand is eroded rock, and it comes in many colors because rocks come in many different colors. Rocks have three main divisions. *Igneous* rocks

8. Why are sands different colors?

were once molten and come from deep inside the earth. They have cooled at different speeds and assume a variety of colors ranging from white, pink, and green to shiny black. The second type, *sedimentary* rocks is formed by layers of sand and clay that are washed down into lake beds and ocean floors. They become cemented under pressure and often are raised up again by later earth movements. Sandstone breaks down easily into sand particles colored red, brown, and yellow. Finally, *metamorphic* rock is formed when rock is changed in form through heat and pressure during periods of deep burial. Slate was once clay, quartzite came from sandstone, and marble is metamorphosed limestone. Again, with these different types of rock come a variety of colors. The next activity has a further discussion on these three types of rocks.

Rocks undergo erosion through the powers of wind, ice, streams, gravity, and trampling. Friction breaks the rock into sand, which then is easily transported to collecting places along the shores of oceans, rivers, and creeks, or left in huge deposits found in deserts.

Sand is chiefly composed of the igneous materials quartz, feldspar, and bits of mica. A mountain's granite is eroded, and rain washes this sand down into the lowlands.

Some beach sands, called basalt rock, were produced by volcanic ash, originally black lava; other sands come from broken shells and coral materials. White sand often comes from broken-down coral rock, and pink sand is usually from sea shells.

Research questions

Information to read aloud and research with your children:

Is a natural sand source near your home or school? Check along riverbanks, lakeshores, in a quarry, or along any beach. Each time you explore a new beach or sand source, collect some in a little jar to note the variety of colors of sand. Why is sand so often found by a water's edge? Are some sands you've found more coarse than others? Using a scale, weigh the different sands you've found to see which weighs more and investigate why. What are some of the human uses of sand?

Indoor or outdoor activity
Time needed: 1 hour
Materials needed:

- ❑ Colored sand (at least 4 different colors)
- ❑ Glue
- ❑ Cardboard
- ❑ Markers
- ❑ Newspaper

1. Before starting, discuss where the jars of sand came from and why the sand is made up of different colors. Explain how the sand is used in the project. If a variety of sand colors is hard to find, or if the colors are not as bright as you would like them, dye the sand different colors. Fill a glass jar two-thirds full of sand. Drip in food dye of the desired color. Close the jar and shake it until most of the sand is the desired color. Spread the sand out on a newspaper until it is completely dry. Pour it back into the jars until you are ready to use it.

2. The children should draw a design on their pieces of cardboard with a dark-colored marker.

3. Work with one color of sand at a time. First, spread glue evenly in one section of the design. Then, over a newspaper, pour one color of sand over that glued section. Press gently on the poured sand with your fingers. Shake any excess sand off onto the newspaper and then pour it back into the proper jar. Continue with the glue and another color of sand, until the whole design has been covered.

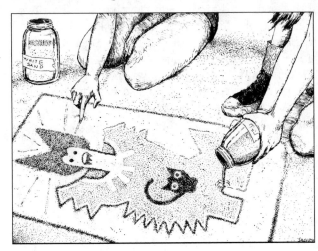

Pouring and drawing with sand is a timeless art that the Native Americans of the Southwest have kept alive.

9. Why do rocks have so many shapes & textures?

Rocks that are round and smooth are often that way because they have been moved and formed by water and ice. Rocks that end up in a river or stream bank get transported and rolled along by the current. This rolling action results in round and smooth river rocks. Some places have large granite slabs of smoothly polished stone. This polishing was done in areas where glaciers advanced more than 50,000 years ago. This evidence of former ice ages is called *glacial polish*.

As stated in the previous activity, rocks are divided into three groups: sedimentary, metamorphic, and igneous. Sedimentary rocks are formed when layers of sand and mud are pressurized together over time. The layers in sedimentary rock are often evident, as in sandstone. Sedimentary rocks are often less dense than metamorphic rocks.

Metamorphic rocks are formed deep within the earth when rocks undergo changes due to intense pressure and heat. Often these rocks are former sedimentary rocks that have been recrystallized due to the heat or pressure. For example, slate is recrystallized shale, marble is recrystallized limestone, and quartzites are recrystallized sandstones. Metamorphic rocks are usually heavy and dense.

Igneous rocks all originate from *magma*, or liquid rock, from within the earth. Some of these rocks cool below the surface, such as granite. This rock is hard and tough, and it often contains many quartz crystals. Other igneous rocks cool above the surface of the earth and are known as volcanic rocks. Two examples of this rock, obsidian and pumice, look very different. Both obsidian and pumice come from volcanoes. Obsidian is shiny, black, and very smooth. Pumice is often light colored, and is so lightweight that it can float on water. The rate at which a rock cools from a liquid state to a solid influences its shape and texture. For example, the most rapid cooling of lava results in the black, glass-like obsidian.

Research questions

Information to read aloud and research with your children:

Begin a rock collection and, using a field guide, determine if your rocks are sedimentary, metamorphic, or igneous. It helps to

use a hand lens when examining rocks up close. Rock collectors often carry a light hammer to help excavate an interesting rock form and a bag to carry specimens home. It is a good idea to keep notes where you gather your rocks to be able to continue learning about the mineral makeup of the earth. Look for rocks in road cuts, cliffs, human excavations, or outcroppings. How many colors of rocks can you find? Which rocks appear harder to break than others? Each time you travel to a new area or state, collect rocks that represent the new area to you.

Indoor or outdoor activity
Time needed: 15–30 minutes
Materials needed:

Rock-n-roll grab bag drawings

- ❏ Sketchbook/journal or drawing paper
- ❏ Found rocks or rocks assembled from rock collections
- ❏ Paper sacks
- ❏ Drawing tools

1. Have the group find rocks that appear interesting or have the children bring together rocks from their personal rock collections.

2. Small groups of three or four children work well for this activity. Collect each group's rocks in a separate sack.

Grab-bag drawing allows the children to draw the many textures found in rocks.

3. Draw the rocks after feeling them without looking at them. With one person holding the sack, two others may reach in at once and feel for a rock and begin to draw it. Take turns drawing until each child has drawn all of the rocks in the bag.

4. After everyone is finished, empty the sacks and see if the children can determine which rock belongs to which drawing.

5. The children will become very aware of the shapes and textures of the rocks using their sense of touch with one hand while drawing with the other.

10. What is in a fossil?

The fossil record is the key to the earth's history. Fossils are the remains and traces of plants and animals that are preserved in the earth's crust. Fossils can be bones, tracks, or tunnels left by ancient life millions of years ago. An organism might become fossilized in one of several situations. The first is by being buried very rapidly, which would slow down decomposition and deter or limit scavengers. In the second, the organism might possess hard parts capable of being fossilized. Freezing can also preserve organisms.

Whenever trees are injured, resin oozes out. Resin is sticky and many insects and spiders were trapped by this resin. Some fossils have been found in pieces of golden amber, a fossilized resin that oozed from trees millions of years ago and then hardened.

Fossils help explain the life forms and the terrain of the earth that existed millions of years ago.

The study of fossils is called *paleontology*. The oldest known forms of life have been recorded in fossils and are microscopic cells believed to be 3.8 billion years old. Fossilized algae has been discovered in rocks that are two billion years old. The

earliest known fossil vertebrates occur in rocks around 500 million years old. The remains of these marine animals are made up of pieces of the bony armor that covered their bodies. Through studying fossils, scientists are able to better understand how successful and diverse the history of life has been on earth.

Information to read aloud and research with your children:

Evolution is the theory that animals and plants have gradually changed shape and form over millions of years to enable them to survive in their surroundings. How can scientists tell what early plants and animals looked like? How can fossils help prove the theory of evolution?

Study any fossil displays in your local museums to learn more about the plants and animals that lived in your region thousands of years ago.

Indoor or outdoor activity
Time needed: 15–30 minutes
Materials needed:

- ❑ Clay
- ❑ Newspaper
- ❑ Cardboard
- ❑ Objects from nature (leaves, shells, fish skeletons, dead insects)
- ❑ Tweezers

1. To make clay impressions, everyone in the group should first prepare a slab of clay by flattening and rolling a fist-size ball of clay into a ½-inch-thick slab.

2. Gather together a variety of leaves, ferns, insects, shells, or any other found object that can be imprinted into the clay.

3. Lay one or more of the objects on the slab and press them gently under a stiff piece of cardboard.

4. Carefully lift off the cardboard. With the tweezers, carefully pull out the nature objects from the clay, and examine the

print that has formed. Experiment with different shapes and arrangements.

5. The clay impression can represent an example of a type of fossil. The clay represents the mud of thousands of years ago. Placing the nature objects in the clay would be similar to ancient organisms making imprints in the mud. If nothing collected in the prints, the mud dried, forming what is now called a *cast fossil*. If sediments filled the imprint, a sedimentary rock formed with the print of the organism on the outside. This type of fossil is called a *mold fossil*.

11. Does nature use glue?

Within nature, many animals and plants rely on the ability to stick or be sticky. Barnacles make the strongest known glue. Scientists know of 800 species of barnacles. All attach themselves for life with their self-made cement to pilings, rocks, hulls, and docks. Paleontologists have found fossils of barnacles similar to today's species that attached themselves to rocks 150 million years ago.

Pine pitch is very sticky. The tree puts out pitch as a scab that forms on any injured part of the tree. Pitch turns into amber, which has a golden-red, glass-like quality.

The inside of a flower is often sticky. As pollen is transported by insects, birds, bats, the wind, and water, a flower's stickiness captures the pollen, enabling potential fertilization.

Many insects make sticky substances to attach their homes to trees or rocks. For example, wasps, bees, and a caterpillar's cocoon employ sticky substances that the insects are able to make themselves. A spider's web uses sticky substances to trap its prey. A frog's tongue is sticky on the end to help catch its fast-moving prey.

Research questions

Information to read aloud and research with your children:

What are the ingredients that make up the glue and paste that we use at home or in our schools? Why are these ingredients sticky? Why does glue or paste stay in a liquid state until it is squeezed out of the bottle? Research and do an investigation as

to what makes glue work. Compare the glues we use to the glues found in nature. How does a barnacle attach itself so firmly to rocks or even whales?

Indoor or outdoor activity
Time needed: 1 hour/4 times a year
Materials needed:

Nature collage

- ❏ Found objects from nature
- ❏ Paper sack
- ❏ Glue
- ❏ 12-x-12-inch square of cardboard
- ❏ Scissors

1. Take a walk and gather objects from nature in paper sacks. After you have gathered objects such as seeds, leaves, rocks, flowers, grasses, cones, and feathers, do the following activity.

Gluing down a nature collage requires the careful handling of plants.

2. Mention that the word *collage* is derived from the French verb *coller*, meaning "to glue." Have the children cut squares of cardboard. Each child should arrange the found objects on the cardboard before they glue the objects down.

3. A border of seeds or beans adds a finished touch to the collage. Arrange the beans around the collage in a repeating pattern and glue them down.

4. Make these collages quarterly and then assemble them all together after one year. Each season's findings will be different. Have the children explain the seasonal changes of their collages.

12. Why do we have wind?

Wind can be compared to the air rushing out of a balloon, going from a high-pressure area to a low-pressure area. Winds do not blow in a straight line from high-pressure areas to low-pressure areas. Because the earth is spinning, the winds are pushed off course. Winds are pushed to the right in the northern hemisphere and to the left in the southern hemisphere.

This spin creates worldwide patterns of winds called *prevailing winds*, or winds blowing from the same direction most of the time. Much of the world's weather depends on this great system of winds that blow in set directions. Just as there are different currents in a water system, the air moves like a fluid and flows in different air currents. Several different weather patterns might occur at the same time in different levels of the atmosphere. The air flows with one pattern in a higher atmosphere and a different one closer to the earth's surface.

Offshore and onshore breezes are examples of different regular winds. Offshore breezes occur when heat rises over the ocean at night, creating a vacuum that is filled by blowing winds that flow into the space. Onshore breezes occur when the heat rises off the land during the day; the breeze returns onto the shore to fill in that void.

Information to read aloud and research with your children:

Many different devices use wind to power them. Have you seen how a wind sock works? You have probably flown a kite before. What can you learn about the wind from flying a kite? Is the wind the same near the ground as higher up in the sky? What is the best kind of day for flying a kite? What do windmills do? Have you heard about or seen the many windmills that are being used to generate electricity in California? How do they work?

Outdoor activity
Time needed: 1 hour
Materials needed:

- ❏ Cotton thread
- ❏ Scissors
- ❏ Found objects from nature

1. Walk outside and stop in a quiet place. Gather materials to construct mobiles. Have the children work in pairs to complete their mobiles. To make the mobiles do the following steps.

2. Tie the objects to the sticks, allowing several inches of thread to hang between each object and the sticks. The children should hold the stick in the middle while hanging the objects, to give a sense of balance to the construction. A mobile should be hanging with a sense of balance, even when a mild breeze causes it to move or rotate.

3. If the mobiles are made entirely from natural objects, have the children find a special spot away from the group and the trail where they can hang their mobile.

4. Perhaps another adventurer will come upon the mobiles, but even if it is not for a long time, each mobile-maker will have a clear image of where his or her mobile is hanging and moving with the breeze as part of the forest.

Research questions

Mobiles from nature

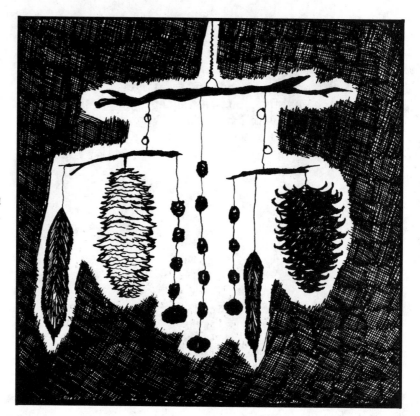

The wind helps to display a balanced hanging mobile.

13. Where do hurricanes & tornadoes come from?

Natural disasters are usually intense and brief and often cause major changes in both human and natural areas. Two natural disasters, hurricanes and tornadoes, are viewed as destructive events because they cause great damage to homes, human lives, and the land as we know it.

Hurricanes are tropical storms in which the wind spirals at speeds of more than 75 miles per hour. They begin over the ocean, when moist, wet air rises very quickly and cooler air rushes in from below. A wall of water some 25 feet high is sucked up by the storm's *eye*, the ring of low pressure at the storm's center. The mass of air spirals, going faster and faster. Giant waves are whipped up by the winds. When hurricanes reach land, they cause great damage. However, hurricanes usually die down quickly once they reach land, because they are removed from the ocean conditions that cause them.

Tornadoes form over land when warm air rises very quickly and cooler air rushes in from below. They are smaller than hurricanes and usually don't last very long. However, they can be stronger than hurricanes and more intense, with winds up to 240 miles per hour. Tornadoes are also referred to as *twisters* and *whirlwinds*. *Dust devils* are formed in the desert by columns of hot air whirling up from the ground. The center of a tornado is also called the *eye*. The air is calm in the eye, but all around it the winds are blowing with terrific force.

Information to read aloud and research with your children:

Research questions

What does a hurricane do to the life below the ocean surface? Can you think of a way to simulate a strong wind above water and experiment to see if the water below the surface is affected? During tornadoes, are burrowing animals in as much danger as animals that live above the ground? Have you witnessed any of these spirals of wind? How does the land look after a natural disaster? What would you do to protect yourself from these strong winds?

Drawing tornadoes or hurricanes

Indoor or outdoor activity
Time needed: 30 minutes
Materials needed:

- ❑ Sketchbook/journal or drawing paper
- ❑ Books or photographs of tornadoes and hurricanes
- ❑ Pencils
- ❑ Markers
- ❑ Drawing boards

1. Discuss the origins and power of hurricanes and tornadoes. Mention where these natural disasters are more geographically likely to occur. Use books and pictures as reference materials for ideas.

2. Draw pictures trying to capture the force of a tornado or hurricane. How would they appear? How do you draw torrential rains or gale-force winds? These pictures are likely to appear abstract.

13. **Where do hurricanes & tornadoes come from?**   29

3. Have the children discuss what the land would look like after the tornado or hurricane passed through. How has nature adapted to survive these natural disasters?

14. Where does snow come from?

For snow to form, a cloud must be chilled to a few degrees above or below 32°F. The cloud droplets are supercooled and freeze together into crystals. Because the crystals carry a thin film of unfrozen water, they mat into snowflakes when they collide. In extreme cold, the crystals are drier and fall as granular snow. Rain that starts in warm air and falls through a cold layer turns not into snow but into ice pellets called *sleet*. *Hailstones* originate as frozen raindrops in high clouds; the raindrops then move through thunderstorms and are hurled about in updrafts, picking up layers of snow and ice.

Mountains are storehouses for falling snow, slowly releasing it down into the lowlands through streams as the spring thaw begins. Sometimes these spring thaws bring floods, depending on how deep a snowfall the winter provided and how warm the spring is.

Snow is an excellent insulator. Many small animals escape freezing winds and subzero temperatures by burrowing under the snow. These animals are called *subnivian*—those which live beneath the snow. The insulating factor of snow also keeps the soil from freezing. If the ground froze, many hibernating species—insects, worms, chipmunks—would die of cold. Snow allows fungi and bacteria to remain active, sometimes all winter, decomposing litter on the ground floor.

Research questions

Information to read aloud and research with your children:

Did you know that regions in southern Canada and the northern United States receive more snow in a year than the North Pole? The high Arctic near the North Pole is actually a frigid desert. But the little snow that does fall, stays.

Did you know that the majority of the five billion people who live on earth never see snow during their entire lives because they live in tropical or mildly temperate climates?

On average, snow is 10 times lighter than water. Fill a pail with snow, bring it indoors, and let it melt. Measure the water equivalent. But before you discover the results guess how much water will be in your bucket after the snow melts. Were you correct?

Outdoor activity
Time needed: 30–45 minutes
Materials needed:

- ❑ Snow
- ❑ Mittens

1. Talk with the children about how different animals survive in the winter. Their various adaptations for survival include camouflage, insulation, thick fur, wide feet, claws, wings, feathers, hibernation, and migration.
2. This activity works well with the children working in groups of three or four. Each group should sculpt an imaginary animal that is perfectly adapted for the immediate environment. They can use a variety of animal adaptations. For example,

Winter-adapted snow sculptures

Making creatures that are perfectly adapted for a snowy climate triggers the imaginations of children.

they might sculpt a creature with a hard turtle shell, wings, and a long trunk to dig beneath the snow for food.

3. Have the children introduce their snow sculpture to the rest of the group. They should be prepared to explain its name, its adaptations for survival, its predators, and its food sources.

15. What is fire ecology?

Fire ecology, or *ecopyrology*, is the study of how fire affects the cycles of an environment. For each different terrain, whether it be forest, sage, chapparal, or an urban area, fire has a different effect. Fire affects the soil, plants, air, water, and animal life of each different community. Usually people think of forest fires as terrible destructive forces. In human terms, it does appear that way. Yet many lightning-generated forest fires can actually be beneficial to plants and animals in the long run.

Fires have always been a part of forests. Many trees have evolved with fires and rely on them to clear land, open seed cones, and rid the ground of old and broken branches. Many trees actually depend on fire for their reproduction. Heat from a fire causes the seed coats to open up permanently, allowing the seeds to be released. Examples of trees and shrubs that rely on fire are the jack pine, lodge pole pine, giant sequoia, manzanita, and the ceanothus. When natural fires are suppressed by human intervention, the whole forest community is greatly altered. For example, without fire, the white fir and Douglas fir gradually replaced the ponderosa pine, which is dependent on the fire's heat. Ceanothus shrubs are a vital food source for elk and deer. If a fire doesn't occur, the ceanothus won't thrive, and the deer and elk's food source declines.

During forest fires, most animals are able to escape injury by simply walking away from it. Burrowing animals are relatively safe underground where the soil protects them from the heat. During forest fires, animal deaths are usually the result of breathing too much smoke. If an animal can get away from a forest fire and smoke, it will likely survive.

Fire is a quick method of decomposition. The blaze releases the nutrients from the plant matter back into the soil very rapidly. A blackened, burnt area is a source of rich new green growth usually within a few years.

Information to read aloud and research with your children:

Is there a site near where you live that had a fire recently? These sites offer wonderful opportunities to witness firsthand the abilities of nature to rebound. Inspect the area two or three times over the course of a year to note the different plants that are able to colonize in the newly opened area. Do you see any growing evidence of wildlife? While it makes us sad when an area appears to be destroyed by a fire, how can fire be actually good in some ways for a forest?

Outdoor activity
Time needed: 30 minutes
Materials needed:

- ❏ Found charcoal (from burnt trees, near railroad tracks, in barbecue pits)
- ❏ Drawing paper
- ❏ Watercolor brushes
- ❏ Drawing boards

1. Take a walk with the children to an area where you know there are available charcoal deposits. Look for pieces of charcoal with which to draw.

Charcoal for drawing can be found in fire pits or on burnt trees.

2. Experiment with the charcoal by drawing lines, shapes, and pictures of the trees the charcoal came from. Rub the charcoal with your fingers to provide shading.

3. After the drawings are finished, experiment using the watercolor brushes and water. This kind of painting is called a *wash*.

4. Discuss how charcoal is made and why it makes an interesting drawing tool.

Plant investigations

WHILE TEACHING in the woods of Yosemite, I integrated trees and plants into many of my lessons. We wove pine needles together while lying in soft summer meadows and talked about how the thin bunches of needles sustained the tall pines. Climbing the low branches of an old apple tree in late autumn, we could scan the open view, the "winter view," only available when the leaves were on the ground for the season. Skiing to a giant sequoia grove in winter, we gathered the sequoia's burly little pine cones, shook them, and mixed the henna-colored particles of sap that would fall from the cones with water and draw with sequoia ink. I was always impressed how the buds, grasses, and leaves go through their cycle of dormancy in winter, only to reawake with radiating beauty in spring. Of course, I had studied and understood the plant's life cycle from texts and classes, but to witness it firsthand, to teach about the plant's adaptations to the seasons with the children, made each day a celebration of change.

All year round you can take a walk out in a nearby yard and observe grasses, seeds, buds, and trees. We often think of plants as a sense of landscape; we enjoy their coolness and colors. Most of the plant world grows just fine without our assistance. Consequently, we do not take the time to appreciate how significant it is for the earth and for ourselves.

Plants are a visible, living link between people and the earth's elements. Plants transform the sun's energy into sugars through photosynthesis to feed themselves. Once eaten by animals, plants indirectly pass the sun's energy on to other life. Because plants are the lowest link in the food chain, they are the most consumed. Plants also help to purify the air we breathe. They offer us oxygen in return for the carbon dioxide that they need to live. Plants hold the soil in place, not allowing the wind or water to erode it; after they die, the decomposition of plants enriches the soil.

35

"Plant investigations" offers many ways for children to observe and understand the plant world that surrounds them. Both green and nongreen plants are explored through drawing activities using fungi, mosses, lichen, and the flowering plants. Trees are investigated through "Drawing an imaginary forest," "Back-to-back leaf drawings," and "Drawing a forest floor still life." Other activities illustrate the many contributions of plants and trees for wildlife and people. The more familiar children become with their local plants and trees, the more they will regard them as an integral part of their world. Plants are likely to be growing right outside your window, so it's time to become better acquainted!

1. What is photosynthesis?

Photosynthesis is the most important process to sustain life on earth. Basically it is an energy-storing phenomenon, taking place in the leaves and other green parts of plants while light is available. The sunlight energy is stored in sugars and starches, which become the food to keep the plant alive.

The upper side of the leaf, the side exposed to the sun, begins the process known as photosynthesis. The green stuff in leaves is called *chlorophyll*, or the green "blood" of plant life. When the sunlight hits the chlorophyll, it smashes open the water molecules; carbon dioxide and oxygen reconstruct these molecules to form the sugars and starches. The tiny particles of solar energy are called *photons*. Every leaf carries on photosynthesis.

Photosynthesis is a process that takes place within all green plants.

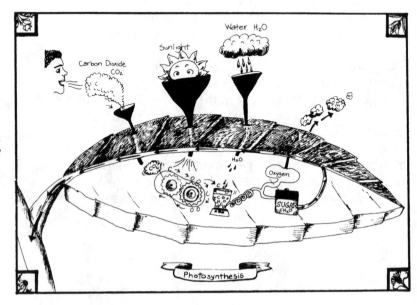

In addition to creating food for the tree, this process also gives off oxygen that is breathed out through the pores of the leaves. This oxygen exhalation freshens the air with new oxygen. People who have large shade trees or live near the woods actually have an oxygen tent overhead. So photosynthesis furnishes raw material: energy and oxygen.

A great deal of photosynthesis takes place in organisms found in the ocean. It is believed that more than 50 percent of the oxygen in our atmosphere originates from the ocean. This fact alone makes it evident why we need to protect our oceans.

Information to read aloud and research with your children:

Research questions

Have you ever studied leaves noticing how they were designed to capture sunlight? Leaves capture as much sunlight as possible in order to carry out photosynthesis as efficiently as possible. You might look at a little leaf and wonder how it can be partially responsible for keeping a great big tree alive. Try estimating how many leaves are on a small tree and then multiply a leaf's surface area times that number. Convert that number to square feet and you might be surprised how much area of sunlight hits a tree. After you have completed the math on a small tree, estimate how many square feet of leaf surface area would be exposed to the sun on a large tree.

Photo paper designs

Outdoor activity
Time needed: 30 minutes
Materials needed:

- ❏ Photo print paper
- ❏ Objects from nature
- ❏ Container of water large enough to soak paper without folding it
- ❏ Pins

Note: Photo paper is available in most craft stores or in the science section of many toy stores. Be sure to store the paper in a cool, dark place; don't expose the paper to light until you are ready to print.

1. After you discuss photosynthesis and the power of the sun, try this photo paper activity. Photo paper is a chemically processed paper that captures the silhouette of any object placed on its surface after being exposed to the sun for a limited period of time. Have the children select a variety of leaves they want to print on the photo paper.

2. If the day is windy, pin the papers down on cardboard. Arrange the leaves on the photo paper in an appealing design. Expose it to the sun for 2 to 5 minutes, depending on the cloud cover.

3. Soak the paper in the water for 1 minute, then dry the paper flat. The images will sharpen during the drying time.

4. Use the photo paper designs to talk about the power of the sun's energy and how leaves conduct photosynthesis. Hang up the finished pictures or arrange them in a collage.

2. Are mushrooms plants?

Mushrooms are definitely plants, but they do not have green chlorophyll and do not convert the sun's energy to food (photosynthesize). Instead, they absorb their food from their surroundings, by sending out fine, silken threads, called *mycelium*, down into other dead plants. All fungi perform this role, and mushrooms are the most famous for their ability to help decompose dead leaf matter and dying trees.

Mushrooms grow rapidly, and within a few days after emerging from the ground, they are capable of giving off millions of spores.

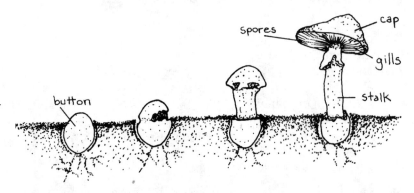

Mushrooms differ from many other plants because, like all fungi, they do not have flowers. Instead of having seeds, they give off *spores* to reproduce themselves.

38   Plant investigations

Mushrooms have many different shapes, colors, and sizes. They are mostly seen in the spring, but can grow year round in many places. Many mushrooms are delicious, and others are extremely poisonous. After picking any mushrooms, you should wash your hands. It is best to not eat any mushrooms growing in the wild unless you are with someone who is a fungi expert. Because they do not require sunlight, mushrooms can grow just as well in the darkness as they do in the light.

Information to read aloud and research with your children:

Research questions

Because of their thin far-reaching mycelium, fungi are the most widespread microorganisms to be found within the forest floor. They have a vital role as decomposers. Can you imagine what a forest would look like if decomposers didn't do their job? Did you ever wonder what happened every year to all the leaves, sticks, animals, and droppings that fell onto the forest floor?

To grow your own mushrooms, take the paper from which you made your spore print (mentioned below) and shake it in your backyard. You will send out hundreds of teensy spores to germinate. Several of them will probably grow to full-grown mushrooms.

Indoor activity
Time needed: Overnight
Materials needed:

**Mushroom
spore prints**

- ❑ Fresh-picked mushroom
- ❑ Knife
- ❑ Black-and-white paper
- ❑ Glass jar

1. Use a field guide to identify and avoid all poisonous types of mushrooms. The umbrella-type mushrooms work best to make spore prints. Mushrooms with white gills print better on dark-colored paper, while those with black gills show up best on light-colored paper.

2. Handle the mushroom very gently. Using caution, cut the stem off flat against the mushroom cap. Place the

mushroom cap on a piece of colored paper, gills down, and cover it with a glass jar.

3. Leave the mushroom covered overnight. The spores will drop from the gills onto the paper. Shake your spore print out in the backyard to grow mushrooms of your own, or, if you want to preserve your spore print, spray it lightly with hair spray from a nonaerosol pump can.

4. Make a variety of these spore prints to discover and learn more about mushrooms.

3. What are lichens?

More than 25,000 species of *lichens* (pronounced "likens") are known. Lichens can be found in a variety of colors: greens, reds, yellows, purples, blacks, oranges, and grays. They also come in a variety of sizes, shapes, and textures. Lichens are often divided into three classifications: crusty, leaf-like, or shrubby.

Lichens are extremely sensitive to air pollution and are used as indicators of air quality. Scientists study both the type of lichens present and the size of the lichens. Shrubby and leaf-like lichens can only survive in clean air. Lichens are relatively rare or nonexistent in large cities and in areas of heavy air pollution. The size of the lichens is also important, with larger lichens meaning better air quality.

Lichens grow very slowly, at a maximum rate of ¼ inch a year. They are capable of living to an age of 4500 years or more. Capable of withstanding terrific hardships, they can be found living on bare rocks in the blazing sun of the desert, in the bitter cold of the arctic and antarctic regions, on trees, or just below the snowline on mountains. Lichens can go without water for a long time by going into a dormant state. During these dormant phases, the environmental extremes do not bother them.

Lichens are often used to describe a symbiotic relationship. That is, lichen is made from a combination of two other plant forms: fungus and algae. The algae supplies the food for both organisms. The fungus protects the algae from harmful light intensities; it also takes in and stores water and minerals for both organisms.

40   Plant investigations

Large mammals such as reindeer and caribou can survive on a type of lichen. Most lichens are not so tasty for humans, and when consumed, might be irritating to the intestines. However, ancient Egyptians ground up one variety of lichens for flour, and the Swedes made bread out of reindeer lichen flour.

Information to read aloud and research with your children:

Research questions

Hand lenses or magnifying glasses work by using lenses and light. A *lens* is usually a thin, circular glass, thicker in the middle, that bends rays of light so that when you look through it an object appears enlarged. Do the lichens appear different through the hand lens than with your naked eye?

Now that you know that lichens are indicators of air pollution, you can do some investigative studies with them.

Does your area have lichens? Using a ruler, measure the size of any lichens that are found. If you went into a local woods or protected area, will you find the same lichens or different ones? What do these results say about the air quality in your area and the outlying area around you?

Outdoor activity
Time needed: 30–45 minutes
Materials needed:

Hand lens or magnifying glass lichen drawing

- ❑ Sketchbook/journal or drawing paper
- ❑ Pencils
- ❑ Lichens
- ❑ Hand lens or magnifying glass
- ❑ Compass or bowl for circle shape
- ❑ Drawing boards

1. Take the children for a walk, equipped with hand lenses or magnifying glasses and drawing tools. Walk to where lichens grow (or fungi, grasses, or leaves if no lichens are available).

2. Select a place for quiet study of the area. Have each person get close to the plant matter with the magnifying tool.

Magnification helps to isolate and study lichens found on rocks.

3. Have each child use a compass or trace an upside-down glass or bowl to draw a circle on the page. Illustrate the lichens or other plant matter that has been magnified, within the circle. The circle shape adds interest to the drawing and repeats the shape of the hand lens or magnifying glass. Remind the children to draw the details of the plants and look under the leaves or stems and inspect for spores.

4. After finishing the drawings, have the children present their circle lichen drawings and mention something they noticed and drew while studying the plants.

4. What are mosses?

Mosses are simple land plants that flourish in damp and shady places. Mosses have a stem with flat leaves branching from it. These leaves are mostly just one cell thick. The stem cells look rather similar to one another, but cells in the center carry water up, and around these cells are cells that carry food

substances. Mosses have no flowers at all. They reproduce by spores, not seeds. The spores are released into the air and travel by way of wind, water, and insects. Spore capsules can be seen, often on the end of long stalks.

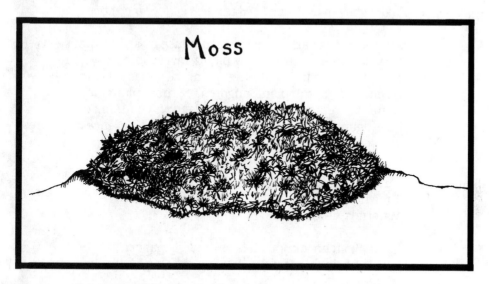

Moss can often be found in damp, cool environments.

Mosses are traditionally thought of as the soft and cool green covering on damp trees, rocks, and along river banks. However, we currently know about 20,000 species of mosses. For example, pygmy mosses appear annually on bare soil after rains and are only 1 to 2 millimeters tall. Pygmy mosses can go through their whole life cycle in a few weeks. The ultragreen, or luminous, mosses—seen around caves and other dark damp places—have an unusual adaptation. The upper surfaces of the cells are curved slightly. This curve serves as a tiny magnifying glass, concentrating the dim light and allowing photosynthesis to occur in an environment that is ordinarily too dark.

Mosses retain moisture, slowly releasing it into the soil. This process helps reduce flooding and erosion. Peat moss is very absorbent. When tested, 2.2 pounds of peat moss takes up and holds 55 pounds of water. Moss also has antiseptic abilities to inhibit bacterial and fungal growth. Often in bogs, peat mosses form floating mats over the water and keep conditions so acidic

4. What are mosses? 43

that the growth of bacteria and fungi is inhibited. Without these decomposers present, dead organisms can be preserved in the water for hundreds or thousands of years.

Research questions

Information to read aloud and research with your children:

As mentioned earlier, mosses reproduce by spores, not seeds. How do spores create a new plant? Investigate how spores differ from seeds. What other plants rely on spores to regenerate? In the plant kingdom, do more plants rely on spores for reproduction or on seeds? Can you think of an investigation that would demonstrate the differences in spores and seeds?

Moss forest drawings

Outdoor activity
Time needed: 30 minutes
Materials needed:

- ❏ Sketchbook/journals or drawing paper
- ❏ Available mosses
- ❏ Pencils
- ❏ Markers
- ❏ Drawing boards

1. After finding an area where mosses are growing, have your children sit or lay next to the mosses with the drawing materials at hand.

2. Each child should pretend they are the size of a tiny bug or caterpillar, imagining and drawing how the moss would appear as they are trying to crawl through it. How tall would the soft stems of the moss appear?

3. Make the drawing cover the whole sheet of paper, to emphasize the enlarged quality of viewing the moss from the size of an insect. An imaginary insect can be included in the drawing.

4. Have the children color in their drawings with markers and hang them up to see the variety of interpretations of the mosses as seen from a different perspective.

Even though most flowering plants are rooted in the ground, they have adapted ways to spread their seeds. The parent plant stays in place, but the flowers contain seeds that can travel in a variety of ways. Some seeds are carried away from the parent plant through the fruit of the plant. When the delicious fruit is eaten, the seeds are passed through an animal's intestines and are deposited away from the parent plant, ready to begin a new life of their own.

Many seeds have ways of hanging onto any passing animal or person. They have tiny barbs that hook onto anything that merely brushes against the plant. Many seeds are sticky in order to stick onto fur or feathers. Other seeds are adapted to be easily transported by the wind. They either have little parachutes, like thistle plant seeds, umbrellas, like dandelion seeds, or wings, like maple tree seeds. Some other seeds travel with water, like the coconut.

5. Why are some seeds & fruits fuzzy, sticky, or delicious?

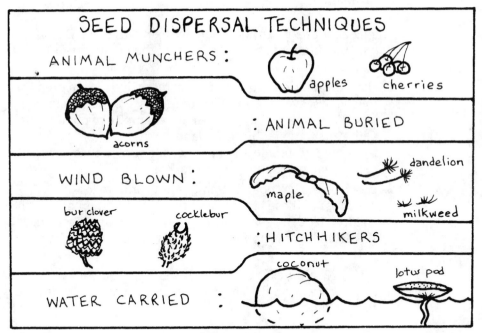

Seeds have adapted a diverse array of dispersal strategies.

Research questions

Information to read aloud and research with your children:

Collect seeds from plants in labeled envelopes while you are out exploring. Try to locate the fruit of the plant. Are all fruits edible? Make a collection of winged, barbed, hooked, and parachuting seeds. Be sure to label each envelope or paper bag carefully with location, date, and species. Some seeds will store only a year or two before they will not germinate; others, like the lotus plant, will still germinate after lying dormant a thousand years!

Scavenger hunt sketch

Outdoor activity
Time needed: 30 minutes–1 hour
Materials needed:

- ❏ Sketchbook/journal
- ❏ Pencils
- ❏ Markers

1. Talk about textures and colors in the plant world. Discuss why the different seeds and fruits of the plant appear the way they do.
2. Have the children work with a partner. Give the children the following scavenger hunt list (or modify it to better suit your area). The children should look for examples of plant seeds and fruits that are: bumpy, round, waxy, resemble a parachute, resemble an umbrella, sticky, soft, fuzzy, hard, red, brown, green, purple, brown, black.
3. Describe the boundaries and the time limit to look for examples of these plant adaptations. Rather than having the children pick the examples they find, have them do a quick sketch and a description of the location of the plant's seeds or fruit.
4. When 20 minutes is up (or whatever time you feel is appropriate), call the group together and have them describe their findings.

6. How does a seed become a plant?

A *seed* contains the embryo of a new plant and the food for the first stages of its growth. A seed *germinates*, or begins to transform itself into a plant, with the aid of soil, sunlight, and moisture.

46   *Plant investigations*

After a seed has germinated it is called a *seedling*. In order for a seedling to survive, it has to have its required amount of sunlight and moisture and enough ground space available to establish its roots. Many seedlings do not survive due to shallow roots, the wrong amount of moisture, or not enough sun; sometimes they do not survive because they are eaten.

If a seedling survives, it will eventually develop the ability to reproduce itself. Many plants, called *annual* and *biennial* species, go through their growth and development phases, then flower and die within one or two years. Others, called *perennials*, are more complex in how they reproduce, and often live for many years.

Information to read aloud and research with your children:

This investigation allows you to witness a seed germinating. Take a paper cup and slice down one side of the cup to the bottom and cut along the bottom about two and a half inches, leaving the other side of the cup intact to act as a hinge. Cover this opening (inside the cup) with plastic wrap. Using clear tape, tape the plastic in place. The paper cup should now have a hinged door that you can open and look into the cup through the plastic wrap. Put a rubber band around the cup to keep the door closed. Fill ⅔ of the cup with soil. Next to the plastic wrap, place some bean seeds or other large seeds. Cover the seeds with a half inch of soil. Punch a few tiny drainage holes in the bottom of the cup with a sharp pencil. Water just enough to keep the soil moist. To witness the seeds germinating, remove the rubber band and open the door to the cup. Keep the door closed except for when observing the seeds. How long would you guess it would take for the seeds to germinate? What color are the roots? Do some of the seeds germinate later than the others? Why? What further discoveries can be made using the seed-witness cup?

Research questions

Devise a science experiment using the seed-witness cup, with different seeds and different amounts of sunlight.

6. How does a seed become a plant?   47

Pressed plants   Outdoor activity and indoor activity
Time needed: At least one hour to make the press and press the
first plants
Materials needed:

- ❑ 2 pieces of pegboard (Masonite with holes in it),
  12×18 inches
- ❑ Newspaper
- ❑ 12-x-18-inch corrugated cardboard (cut from any
  cardboard box)
- ❑ Rope or straps to tighten the press
- ❑ Plants from nature

1. Have the children help make a permanent reference
   collection of plants from different habitats that you explore.
   Be sure to gather specimens only where collecting is
   permitted, and never take exotic or rare plants. Only take a
   few plants at time, and only where there are so many that a
   few would not be noticed.

2. Dig up the entire plant. If the plants are too large, take a
   small piece of bark and a twig with leaves. Place collected
   plants in a moistened plastic bag to keep them fresh until
   you get home.

3. To preserve your plants, you could construct a plant press.
   Use two pieces of Masonite or pegboard (board with holes in
   it). A good size is 12×18 inches. Place the plants between two
   sheets of newspaper. Layer plant "sandwiches" with
   corrugated cardboard, and place them between the two cut
   sheets of pegboard. Use straps or rope to press the plants by
   tightly securing them.

4. Plants can also be effectively pressed by laying several sheets
   of newspaper on the bottom of a cardboard box. Place the
   plants down flat (not overlapping one another) on the
   newspaper. Lay several sheets of newsprint on top of the
   flowers, followed by a layer of cardboard, and finally, heavy
   books or bricks.

5. After about a month, when the plants are dried and pressed,
   mount the plants to heavy white sheets of paper using small
   paper strips glued at each end. Label each sheet with the

common and scientific name, date, place collected, and your name. The plants, flowers, and ferns will be pressed with the majority of color intact.

6. Store the pressed sheets flat in a cabinet or a file box. These pressed plants can be used as reference materials in order to understand the structure of plants. The pressed plants can be drawn in detail for scientific illustrations.

7. Why do plants have flowers?

Many plants are remembered best for their flowers. Plants have flowers to make sure that the plant reproduces successfully. They contain the male and female reproductive parts that produce seeds from which new plants grow. The two sexual organs of a flower are a part of their structure. The female *carpel* has a seed-containing *ovary* at its base and pollen-catching *stigmas* topping the slender supporting *style*. The carpel receives the pollen and holds the seeds, enabling them to be fertilized and to mature. The male *stamen* is made up of two parts: the thin *filament* and the pollen-producing *anther*. Both the carpel and stamens are encircled by the petals, which are in turn surrounded by the sepals. The *sepals* are the original parts of the bud that protected the young flower before it was ready to open.

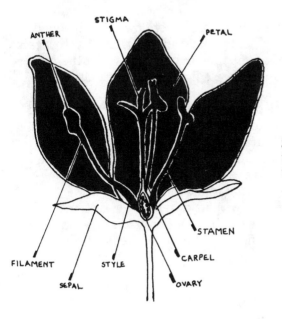

Sit with a child and take the time to try to identify the parts of a flower.

We enjoy flowers because they are colorful and often smell sweet. Flowers' colors and scents are not intended for people, but rather for the insects, birds, and bats that pollinate them. It has been discovered that flowers can appear quite different to pollinators than they do to us. We do not perceive light energy in the ultraviolet range, but many insects, particularly bees, do. Often, the patterns found on flowers leading into the sexual parts of the blossom are like landing pads that guide and steer the pollinators to receive nectar and exchange pollen. Flowers that are pollinated by flies are rarely sweet-smelling, but rather smell like dead meat, or carrion.

Flowers that rely entirely on the wind for pollination are usually small and less showy in color because they do not have to attract insects. Because they do not have colors and perfume to attract the insects for pollination, they have adapted with a mass of pollen much greater than other flowering plants. This vast amount of pollen usually gets released in the early spring before leaves block their way. People with hay fever are aware of this pollen distribution each spring as the wind transports it and triggers their allergies.

Research questions

Information to read aloud and research with your children:

Compound flowers have a small cluster of flowers in the middle, although *simple flowers* contain no center clusters. Try to locate a simple flower and a compound flower and dissect them to note their differences. In simple flowers (such as buttercups and petunias), note how the sepals make up the outer circle with the petals inside of them. Note the stamens, which look like a ring of little knobs, each on a stalk. In the center is the *pistil.* Did you know that compound flowers look like tiny bouquets when examined closely? Compound flowers include daisies, black-eyed Susans, asters, thistles, and chrysanthemums. Note that in the middle of the flower, each floret is a separate flower with its own pistils and stamens that has been packed together with other florets. As you continue to examine flowers in the field, note to see if the flowers are simple or compound flowers.

Outdoor or indoor activity
Time needed: 45 minutes
Materials needed:

- ❏ Sketchbook/journal
- ❏ Drawing paper
- ❏ Colored pencils
- ❏ Drawing boards

1. Study different flowers, either in a meadow or flower garden. Or bring together different flowers in a jar of water. Have each person select a flower to draw. Use the colored pencils and sketchbooks and illustrate the flower, noting if it is a simple or compound flower, its shape, color, and sexual parts.

2. Draw for just three minutes, then signal for the group to rotate to another flower.

3. After five or six rotations, have the group assemble and discuss their drawings. Did anyone notice any landing platforms on the flowers, any distinct odors, or any flowers that appeared to be night bloomers?

4. One fun thing to do later is to try to observe the night pollinators. Wrap red cellophane over a flashlight to observe night bloomers' pollinators without disturbing them.

8. What are weeds?

Although *weeds* are defined as plants growing where they are not wanted, they can be beautiful and interesting to observe. Weeds are wild flowers, as they are rarely cultivated. Weeds grow in both normal and adverse situations; you might see a weed growing from cracks in the sidewalks, a junked car in a vacant lot, or within rain gutters. Many grow quickly and send their seeds out in stickery fashion. As we become better acquainted with them, weeds can help us understand the adaptability and ways of success within the plant kingdom.

The common dandelion is a true measure of success. Dandelions seem to be able to grow almost everywhere; they are common not only in lawns but also in meadows, pastures, and along the roadsides. Along with the dandelion, red clover is a weed with a successful rate of survival. It is a favorite among

butterflies as their long tongues can reach the deep nectar wells, but only the burly bumblebees are successful at being able to reach the pollen. Therefore, bumblebees are the chief pollinators for red clover. Both red clover and dandelions are quite common and easy to observe.

Research questions

Information to read aloud and research with your children:

Can you find a dandelion and determine why it is so successful in the plant kingdom? Note its structure, its flower, and its seeds. It has a thick fleshy root that penetrates deeply into the ground, far below where heat and dryness can affect it. Do you think rabbits, moles, or grubs can easily break through the thick stem to eat at its base? Its large, hollow stem is able to bend in the wind better than any plant that has a more compact stem. It secretes a bitter, milky juice that keeps grazers from bothering it. After the dandelion loses its golden flower, what type of seed does it generate?

Conduct a plant inventory within a city block to identify as many weeds or wild flowers as you can find. What plants are the easiest to find? Do more weeds grow where it is sunny or where it is shady? Does any place have a noticeable number of different kinds of weeds?

Growing and drawing weeds

Outdoor activity
Time needed: 1 hour
Materials needed:

- ❑ Pair of envelopes
- ❑ Pencils
- ❑ Markers
- ❑ Old rough socks
- ❑ Paper cups
- ❑ Soil
- ❑ Pebbles

1. We are all familiar with the beautiful seed packages sold every spring for flowers and vegetables. Weeds deserve beautiful seed packages, too! In this activity, you will make seed packages deserving for our friend, the weed.

2. Note the plants in a weedy field from mid-summer through the fall. Study and draw a picture of the flowers of several different weeds, each one on the front of an envelope. Color the envelopes with markers.

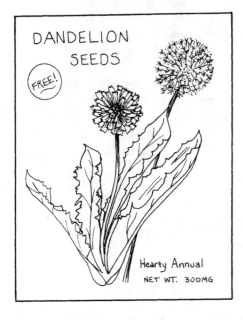

A dandelion is a common, hardy weed that uses the wind to help disperse its tiny umbrella-like seeds.

3. Gather seeds from the weeds by picking them off your pants or by taking a walk with your shoes off in a pair of old rough socks. Your socks will pick up a number of seeds. Also, many weed seeds are wind-pollinated, such as dandelion seeds. Simply blow their seeds into your envelope.

4. After taking your walk and picking off the seeds, store the seeds in the envelope that has the picture of the plant that you believe the seed originated.

5. Upon returning home, plant the seeds in paper cups with soil in them. Moisten the soil and then stick three or four of the same seeds in each cup about a half inch into the soil. Water the plants every two days. See what kind of weeds develop.

6. Match the growing plants with the sketches you made on the seed envelopes. See if you guessed right as to what weeds would emerge from the different seeds.

8. What are weeds?   53

9. Why do plants & trees have leaves?

Leaves supply nourishment that allows a plant or tree to carry on all of its life processes. Soon after they unfold, the new young leaves take on the job of making food. Leaves produce food by using the energy from the sun to combine raw materials drawn from the soil and air. This process is called photosynthesis. The basic ingredients that a plant needs for photosynthesis are carbon dioxide, water, and, of course, sunlight.

Most leaves are flat and wide to catch the most sunlight. The veins in a leaf are very important as they carry water through the leaf and also send the sugars down into the rest of the tree. Leaves have highly modified structures and their shape and arrangement are important clues in identifying different plants.

Leaves on trees create shade. Shade provides for as much as 20°F difference of temperature in an area. Tree leaves are a passive energy source, because in the summer they provide shade to cool an area, and in the winter they are shed, exposing the area to the sun's warmth.

Research questions

Information to read aloud and research with your children:

In the winter, most green plants and many trees cannot continue to function because their food-making processes depend upon sunlight and moisture. When plants stop photosynthesizing, the chlorophyll, or green-making part, begins to decrease. Chlorophyll is so intense that, during the summer months, it actually hides the other colors that are present in leaves. As the chlorophyll disappears, the yellows and oranges of the leaves are revealed. The reds that develop are a result of a chemical change that occurs in plants. Do some research to discover what this chemical change is. Explore what the weather conditions must be to achieve the beautiful reds found in some trees. Chart the color changes in various trees and shrubs in a small section beginning in September. Keep track of the types of vegetation, weather, day length, and color changes.

Start a leaf collection and organize it by leaf shape and arrangement. From your leaf collection, what do you conclude

is the best structural design to maximize photosynthesis? Observe the arrangement of leaves on any plant. What do you conclude about their placement on the stem? Notice how different plant leaves repel water. Do certain leaves have a fuzz on the tops of their leaves? Why? Are some leaf surfaces waxy or sculptured to funnel water to or away from the plant? Use a spray bottle to mist leaves and observe the water droplets.

Indoor or outdoor activity
Time needed: 20 minutes
Materials needed:

❑ Sketchbook/journal or drawing paper
❑ Pencils
❑ Assortment of leaves
❑ Drawing boards

1. This activity works well using partners. One person from each pair should choose a leaf, keeping it hidden from his or her partner.

2. Sit back to back with one person holding the leaf and the other person preparing to draw.

Back-to-back leaf drawings

Children will notice the intricate structure of the leaves they observe during back-to-back leaf drawing.

9. Why do plants & trees have leaves?   55

3. The person holding the leaf should describe it by saying how big it is, what its shape resembles, what color it is, and what it feels like.

4. While listening to this description, the drawing partner illustrates what he or she hears.

5. Compare the drawing and leaf. Switch roles, and repeat this activity.

6. Discuss what it felt like to be the describer and what it felt like to be the artist. Who had to observe more closely?

10. How do coniferous & deciduous trees differ?

The *deciduous*, or broad-leafed trees, are part of the earth's dominant group of plants: the flower bearers. Their seeds develop in the fruit of the flower. On the other hand, the needle-bearing *coniferous* trees' seeds develop in the cones on the tree.

Many conifers are shade-intolerant, meaning they prefer to grow in direct sunlight. They grow fast and tall. Many deciduous trees, such as oaks, are shade-tolerant, meaning that they can grow in areas with more shade.

Conifers are one of the oldest plant families. They were growing before the deciduous trees even evolved. Within the conifer family are found the world's most massive living things, the giant sequoias. The conifers definitely hold the record over the deciduous trees in height. Most deciduous trees do not grow over 180 feet. Many conifers grow from 250–350 feet tall. Conifers grow quicker and taller than deciduous trees because they keep their needles year-round, so they carry on photosynthesis year-round.

Deciduous trees evolved as an improvement over coniferous trees. One of the main advantages are the trees' large leaves, as compared to needles, that carry on photosynthesis during the warmer months. The leaves then drop off during cold weather when the days are shorter to avoid water loss and frost damage. Also, the structure of the wood of deciduous trees allows a much freer and stronger sap flow. This sap flow allows the leaves to be able to evaporate more water, photosynthesize quicker, and get more value out of the summer sun. Without any leaves to carry on photosynthesis, deciduous trees do little to no growing in the winter.

Deciduous and Coniferous Trees

In the summer, the forest appears mostly green, but in the fall, the leaves of deciduous trees change colors and fall to the ground.

Conifers have about 650 species. Some of the most familiar are pines, firs, spruces, hemlocks, cedars, larches, and cypresses. Some familiar deciduous trees are elms, walnuts, beeches, oaks, birches, alders, willows, poplars, cottonwoods, aspens, and fruit trees.

Information to read aloud and research with your children:

Research questions

Take a trip into a forest and try to locate and identify any deciduous (broadleaf) trees and conifer trees. Do the trees in the forest appear to be different ages, with some old trees and some young trees? A diverse forest community should have trees that are a variety of ages. Do the trees appear to be in rows? If the trees are in rows, do you think that these trees

were probably planted, rather than having grown wild? How do the seeds of these mixed forests arrive on the ground? Can you locate any seeds? What trees dominate the makeup of the forest, conifers or deciduous?

Gather cones from different types of conifers. Try to gather some cones that have not released their seeds. If you leave the closed cones on the window sill, they will eventually open and their seeds can be easily shaken out. Gather some deciduous seeds, such as acorns from an oak tree. Compare the two types of seeds. What similarities and differences do you note?

Drawing an imaginary forest

Outdoor and indoor activity
Time needed: 1 hour
Materials needed:

- ❑ Sketchbook/journal
- ❑ Pencils
- ❑ Access to a forested area
- ❑ Tree key or tree field guide

1. Have everyone in the group explore and become familiar with four different species of trees using the tree key or field guide; preferably two deciduous trees and two conifer trees. Note and illustrate the bark, leaf structure, and overall size of the trees.

2. Either back home or while still in the forested area, draw a forest in which the four newly learned trees are featured. Try to include as many of the features of the trees as possible— for example, the bark's texture, the tree height, the leaf structure, the flower, the seed or fruit, and animals that frequent the trees.

3. A different twist to the imaginary forest activity is to draw it as from the eyes of a soaring hawk, looking down from above. Include the tops of the four types of trees, along with rivers, animals, hills, valleys, and meadows.

11. What is leaf litter?

Leaf litter, or *duff*, is the organic material on the forest floor. Leaf litter includes leaves, branches, needles, animal droppings,

decomposed trees, dead animals, water, and air. As leaf litter decomposes, it mixes with minerals to help form the top layer of soil, called *topsoil*. Leaf litter is broken down to form soil by bacteria, fungi, and saprophytes. These types of vegetation do not depend on photosynthesis and chlorophyll to live. They obtain energy instead from decaying organic matter found in the leaf litter or immediately below it.

Leaf litter largely originates from materials deposited from trees. In this way, trees help to make their own soil by depositing leaves, branches, and bark onto the forest floor. After the tree dies, it becomes a part of the forest floor layer that is decomposed by bacteria to form soil. This soil then, in turn, provides the necessary germination layer for a new tree to begin its life.

Drawing leaf litter reveals that the forest floor is made up of leaves, pine cones, feathers, sticks, and more.

Leaf litter acts as an insulator to keep the ground from freezing. This insulating layer protects the tiny life-forms living just below the surface of the forest. Leaf litter also helps hide new seedlings from hungry animals.

Information to read aloud and research with your children:

Have you ever considered how trees improve the soil? One way to investigate this is by digging a 1-foot hole through the leaf litter and into the soil within a forest and another 1-foot hole in an

Research questions

adjacent open field. Examine the differences in the soil in the two sites. Using a hand lens, note the differences in the earthworm populations, insect populations, fungus growth, and the organic matter in the soil. Are there other differences? Which soil do you think is receiving more nutrients? How are the trees responsible for this? Investigate the differences in the soil within a conifer forest and a deciduous forest and see if you notice a difference there as well. Be sure to fill your holes back up.

Drawing a forest floor still life

Indoor or outdoor activity
Time needed: 30 minutes
Materials needed:

- ❏ Sketchbook/journal or drawing paper
- ❏ Pencils
- ❏ Leaf litter
- ❏ Drawing boards

1. Pick up objects found on the forest floor such as pine cones, decaying leaves, sticks, animal bones, scat, or pine needles. Place the objects together in an arrangement called a *still life*.

2. Have the group encircle the still life and prepare to draw.

3. Each child should draw the arrangement without looking at the paper. Encourage the children to keep their eyes on the still life at all times, and not on the paper, while drawing.

4. The children's curiosity will be very high as to what their drawing looks like, but try to encourage them to keep working without looking. If any pencils run off the page, tell the children to put them back on the paper where it feels right.

5. When finished, usually in about 5 to 10 minutes, turn the drawing over, still without looking.

6. A second drawing should be done on the other side of the paper. For the second drawing, look back and forth from the paper to the still life. This drawing usually takes about twice as long and demands a more self-critical concentration.

7. When finished, compare the two drawings. Which drawing did they feel they "saw" the still life better? And which one did they enjoy doing better? What did they learn about the elements in leaf litter by doing these drawings?

Trees have bark as a protective strategy against insects, fire, and weather. Bark also acts as an insulator against freezing ice and snow. Bark has a variety of thicknesses. It frequently attains a width of 3 inches or more in conifers, and in extreme cases, such as the giant sequoia, it can even reach 3 feet in thickness. The cracks, or *fissures*, in bark have pockets of tissue that allow a gas exchange to occur between the air and the interior of the stem. Under the hard crusty layer of bark on a tree exists the *phloem*. As the phloem gets older and crushed toward the outside of the tree, it contributes in making the bark. The younger layers of the phloem transport sugars from the leaves to various parts of the tree.

Bark has been used in a variety of ways by people and wildlife. The sugar content of the phloem was recognized by many Native American tribes. Some tribes stripped it from Douglas fir trees and used the dried strips as food for winter and emergencies. Native Americans made a poultice for scrapes and cuts by pounding the hemlock's inner bark. A dull red dye can be obtained from the younger bark of the Eastern hemlock, which is also a source of tannin for shoe leather. Some fibers in barks are used to make ropes. As far as providing for wildlife, bark supplies a partial diet for mice, squirrels, and deer. Bark also provides shelter for many insects, woodpeckers, tree frogs, and spiders.

The bark of a giant sequoia tree is surprisingly soft and spongy.

Research questions

Information to read aloud and research with your children:

The bark protects the tree from fire, insects, storms, and most damage. Many trees experience the hazards of nature, but their bark helps them to survive. Within the protective shelter of the bark, the history of a tree is recorded within the *heartwood*. Within the heartwood, tree rings can tell a great deal about the tree's life history. Each spring and summer, a tree adds new layers of wood to its trunk. The wood formed in the early part of the growing season grows rapidly, and is lighter in color because it consists of large cells. At the end of the growing season, the growth is slower; therefore the wood is darker coming from small cells. The tree experiences very little growth during the winter months. So when the tree is cut, or an increment borer is used to extract a sample of the wood, the layers appear as alternating rings of light and dark wood. Count the dark rings to determine the age of the tree. What do you imagine it means when there are some larger light rings than others? Do you see any evidence of fire scars?

Bark rubbings

Outdoor activity
Time needed: 30 minutes
Materials needed:

- ❑ Paper
- ❑ Crayons
- ❑ Access to a variety of trees
- ❑ Tree key or tree guide

1. This activity is a good one to do with a partner. The partners should select a tree with a texture they find interesting.

2. While one child holds a sheet of paper and presses it against the tree, the partner should take a crayon and rub it firmly, making a steady shading motion on the paper. The relief from the tree bark should show up as a bark rubbing that matches the texture of the tree.

3. Have the partners label what kind of tree the rubbing came from or, if not sure of the tree's type, look it up in a tree guide.

4. Rotate to another kind of tree and repeat the activity, with the children changing roles. Experiment with different colors of crayons.

5. After the children return home, encourage them to put borders on their tree rubbings and hang them up. Discuss with the children the variety of textures of the tree bark, and why the trees have bark and how it helps the tree.

13. What is forest succession?

Forest succession is the rather orderly change that occurs in tree species with the passing of time. For example, if a large oak and pine forest experiences a fire, and a 100-acre block of it is burned to the ground, *succession* is the term used to describe the stages of regrowth of the forest. In this example, the pines will enter a burned clearing before the oaks because pine seeds can be easily blown by the wind from the surrounding forest. Also, pines prefer direct sunlight, whereas oaks grow fine in more shaded areas. Eventually, acorns will be brought into the new pine forest by squirrels and birds, and oaks will be introduced.

Once both species of the trees are growing, the pines will grow more rapidly and to a greater height than the oaks. The pines' height presents no problem to the oaks because the oaks are shade-tolerant. Oaks live longer than pines and will actually dominate the forest after the pines start dying due to natural causes. Perhaps the forest will remain stable, or perhaps another fire will occur. At any rate, through succession, the plants and trees that are the best suited to a situation will grow.

Information to read aloud and research with your children:

Research questions

Visit areas recently cleared of vegetation. Record which plants are the first to grow in the clearing. How did these plants get there? Which plants grow best in open areas where you live? Do you think these sun-loving plants will stay on in the clearing or will another type of plant or tree eventually take its place? How would an understanding of succession influence human decisions on how to protect or use a forest?

Drawing a succession transect

Outdoor activity
Time needed: 45 minutes
Materials needed:

- ❑ Sketchbook/journal or drawing paper
- ❑ Pencils
- ❑ Drawing boards
- ❑ Tape measures or 20-foot pieces of string marked off in foot increments
- ❑ Cleared area

1. Have you ever discovered a circle of trees in a forest before? Often this occurs when a large tree has died and left a *gap* or open area encircled by mature trees. If you can find a gap area, terrific! However, any cleared area surrounded by larger vegetation will serve to demonstrate succession.

2. Have the group encircle the cleared area. Have the children work with a partner. Each pair should have a measuring device. Begin your transect inside a highly forested or vegetated area about 20 feet from the edge of the clearing. Let the children know they have 5 or 10 minutes to draw the major plants and vegetation that they observe.

While conducting a transect, you might discover interesting forms of fungus.

3. Signal for each of the teams to measure 20 feet heading towards the edge of the cleared area. They should then draw the plants that are located at the edge of the clearing. Measure another 20 feet into the cleared area and draw a third picture of the vegetation that grows there.

4. Have each team display their three drawings of the plants and trees they noticed and discuss which teams noticed the same plants. Identify any plants or trees that the group already knows. Use a tree key to help discover the identity of the different plants. Talk about how the different plants need different amounts of sunlight to survive. Discuss how the clearing might change if the smaller plants on the edge grow larger and spread their seeds into the clearing.

14. How do trees benefit wildlife?

All wildlife requires food, shelter, water, and space to complete their habitats. The flowers, fruit, leaves, and seeds from trees provide many species of wildlife with food. The multitude of acorns and other seeds that come from trees are referred to as *mast*. Mast is provided by trees to ensure regeneration of the tree, but is also a main source of food for squirrels and other small rodents. The insects that live in trees are food for many animals higher in the food chain. After trees die, trees are infested by termites and other decomposers.

Trees provide shelter for insects, birds, squirrels, and many species of snakes and frogs. When trees have cavities in them or are dead and still standing (*snags*), they provide shelter for more species of wildlife than when they were still growing and intact. Many birds only nest in a hollow cavity, and are not able to nest successfully without snags. Many hibernating animals or species that go into a dormant state in the winter use snags and tree cavities as places to hole up.

When forests are cut down, wildlife habitat is destroyed. The destruction of habitat is the primary reason for the extinction of animal species today. Many birds are migratory, spending half of the year in warmer regions. The birds' habitat must be in place upon their return or they will not be able to survive. People need to be aware of wildlife habitat before they plan to harvest timber. Large protected areas need to be in place permanently for wildlife species to thrive.

Research questions   *Information to read aloud and research with your children:*

During a walk in the field during the winter months, note how many bird's nests you can find. They will be vacated during the winter months. When you return in the spring, see if birds are using these or other nests. Why is it harder to see birds' nests in the summer than in the winter?

On a dead tree, peel back some of the bark and see if you can find burrowing insects at work. Often you can find beautiful patterns left in the bark by the insects.

Drawing a tree hotel   Indoor or outdoor activity
Time needed: 30 minutes
Materials needed:

❑ Sketchbook/journal or drawing paper
❑ Pencils
❑ Markers

1. Discuss how trees benefit wildlife. This activity works well when the children draw with a partner.

2. Have the partners develop a list of animals that rely on trees for food and shelter. Next, have them draw a picture of their "tree hotel." A tree hotel would be a picture illustrating all of the animals on their list within or around a tree.

3. Break away from stereotypical tree shapes by encouraging the partners to do their drawings outdoors while looking at a tree, or while looking out the window at a tree. Mention to the children that they might include the roots of the tree.

4. Encourage them to include insects, reptiles, mammals, and birds. Pull out field guides or wildlife magazines if the children want to use some references for picture ideas.

5. Hang the pictures up for display and have the children discuss their tree hotel pictures.

This nine-year-old's interpretation of a tree hotel reveals the wonderful habitat provided by a snag.

Jenna Hallas

14. How do trees benefit wildlife?   67

15. How do plants help people?

Plants help people in myriad ways. For example, plants supply oxygen in the air that we need to breathe. Plants are able to store pollutants and carbon dioxide, thereby purifying the air cycle. Plants supply people with food in the form of fruits, vegetables, nuts, and spices. Many plants are eaten by animals (such as cattle, pigs, chickens, and sheep) that provide us with many of our other food sources.

The planting of crops, or *agriculture*, has been the key for the survival of the earth's large human population. Native Americans required a hunting-gathering area of over 10 square miles per person. If one figures the inhabitable earth surface as being 30 million square miles, the natural food capacity would never be able to feed the 5½ billion people living on the earth today. Plant research is carried out in laboratories all over the world. Agricultural experiment stations are fundamental tools for the improvement of agriculture in almost every country.

A few of the many other uses of plants besides for oxygen and food are fibers, beverages, drugs, oils, resins, tannins, cork, rubber, and lumber. Wood is used for many products, including railroad crossties, barrels, firewood, furniture, fence posts, boat building, panelling, flooring, and paper manufacturing.

Of all the hundreds of thousands of plants in existence, actually only a few thousand have been used by people. If wild plants are destroyed to make room for human needs, we will have lost a priceless reservoir for future crop improvements and medicines. It is impossible to know which plants might help sustain people during the next thousand years. This reason shows the importance of preserving large tracts of land in their original state, because we will never be able to replace them once they are destroyed.

Research questions

Information to read aloud and research with your children:

What plants are used in your everyday life? Consider how plants are used in your food, clothing, homes, school books, and medicines. Make a list of all the uses of plants that you encounter in one week. Investigate what life would be like without the use of plants. What part of the world houses the most plants? The

basics that plants require to live are sunlight, moisture, and soil. Plants also need clean air, pollinators, and space to grow. How have people influenced the basic needs of plants?

Indoor activity
Time needed: 30 minutes
Materials needed:

- ❏ Newspaper
- ❏ Water
- ❏ 6–8-inch-deep plastic tub
- ❏ Duct tape
- ❏ Window screen (enough to fit into the bottom of the pan)
- ❏ Wire cutters to cut the screen
- ❏ Wooden picture frame to hold window screen
- ❏ Blender
- ❏ An iron

(I recommend getting the blender, iron, and picture frame from a second-hand shop, and keep them for use on other art projects.)

1. Tear up one piece of newspaper into tiny pieces (½×½ inch). Soak the shredded newspaper in the blender three-quarters full of water for 5 minutes.

2. Cut the wire screen and place it so that it is flush with one side of the frame and use duct tape to adhere it.

3. Add a few blueberries or strawberries to the soaking paper to add color to your paper. Blend the paper and water until it turns into pulp, which looks like very wet mush. Start the blender on low and, after about 15 seconds, run it another 15 seconds on high.

4. Pour the pulp into the plastic tub and repeat the above process until there is enough pulp to submerge the screened frame at least 1 inch. Depending on the size of your plastic tub, it will usually take at least 3 blenders full to begin. Mix the pulp thoroughly with your hand.

5. Lower the framed screen into the plastic tub with the flushed screened part facing up and hold it by the sides for about 4 seconds. Lift the screen up, holding it level, and let

all the water drip back into the tub. The pulp will be laying on top of the screen.

6. Balance the screen on the edge of the tub. Let the water drip back into the tub.

7. Flip the screen onto a newspaper, so that the recycled paper is face down on the newspaper. Gently blot the pulp through the screen with a sponge, removing as much of the liquid, especially from the corners and sides, as you can. Continue blotting until the sponge will no longer take up water. Carefully peel off the screen; if the paper has been blotted thoroughly, the recycled paper will adhere to the newspaper.

8. Close the opened newspaper carefully over the recycled paper and use a warm iron to dry it. Gently blot with the iron (do not rub) on the paper. You will see a considerable amount of steam rising as the paper dries. If the iron is sticking to the newspaper, put a piece of cloth over the newspaper. Turn the paper over and continue drying the paper by blotting it with the iron.

9. When the newsprint is completely dry, your recycled paper can be peeled off. Use a dull knife to catch a corner of your recycled paper and peel it away from the screen. If your paper comes out too thin or with holes in it, add some more paper to the pulp mixture for your next sheet.

16. Why should we care about tropical rain forests?

Even though many of us live thousands of miles away from the equator, where the majority of tropical rain forests are found, our lives are enriched by them daily. Many of the foods we enjoy, including bananas, chocolate, and coffee, are grown in the tropics and are pollinated by insects, birds, and bats from the nearby tropical rain forests. These tropical foods have plant relatives still growing in the forests.

Products developed from tropical forests include rubber, house plants, woods, and oils. People have just begun to tap into the 90,000 plant species available in the forests of the tropics to develop new products.

Drugs to treat cancer, heart disease, ulcers, and asthma—plus thousands of other health concerns—have been found in tropical forests. When you receive medicine from the

pharmacy, the chance that it originated from a tropical rain forest is one in four.

The trees of the tropical rain forest absorb carbon dioxide, maintaining the temperature of the earth. When trees are cut down, carbon dioxide is released, warming the earth by holding the sun's energy close to the earth's surface. This is called the *greenhouse effect.*

Over half of the earth's plant and animal species live within tropical rain forests, even though the forests only take up an eighth of the earth's surface. Many North American songbirds migrate to tropical rain forests in the winter. They cannot live without their warm wintering habitat.

The diversity of plant and animal species in the tropical rain forest needs to be protected.

16. Why should we care about tropical rain forests?   71

The fate of the tropical rain forests is something that touches each of our lives personally. We are connected with the forests in the foods we eat, in many of the products we use, the medicines that help us stay well, the air we breathe, and the animals and plants we enjoy learning about. Not only should we care about the forests for ourselves, but many people live within and nearby the forests who depend on them and who are affected by the soil erosion and water pollution that the removal of the forests causes.

Research questions

Information to read aloud and research with your children:

Tropical rain forests only have two seasons: the rainy season and the dry season. It never freezes and snows there. Temperatures rarely dip below 70°F and often tip the scale at about 85°F. These moderate temperatures remain virtually the same all year round. Many rain forests receive several hundred inches of rain a year. How does your area compare in temperature and rainfall with a tropical rain forest? How would the tropical warm, wet weather influence plant growth? If it never freezes, do you imagine that plants would continue to grow all year round in the tropics?

Tropical rain forest scratch drawing

Outdoor or indoor activity
Time needed: 30 minutes
Materials needed:

- ❏ Drawing paper
- ❏ Crayons
- ❏ Toothpicks
- ❏ Pictures of tropical rainforest plants and animals

1. Within tropical rain forests, much of the sunlight is blocked by the thick canopy layer of the trees and the result is that it can be quite dark under the canopy. This drawing activity will simulate the many colors of the tropical rain forest found under the dark canopy layer of the trees.

2. Each child should cover the entire sheet of drawing paper with many bright colors. Then, color over the entire sheet with a black crayon, obscuring the colors.

3. Looking at pictures of animals and plants of the tropical rain forests, have the children use a toothpick to scratch a drawing through the black crayon, so that the colors will radiate on the paper. Include orchids, kapok trees, butterflies, toucans, parrots, jaguars, and monkeys.

4. Let these pictures serve as reminders of the many reasons why we should be concerned about the fate of the tropical rain forests.

Animal explorations

CHILDREN LOVE close encounters with wildlife and often want to learn more about animals after observing them. The deer in Yosemite have little fear of being hunted, and they often strolled right by a group of awestruck children as we were drawing or having some quiet time. Invariably when we were talking or eating a meal, I would look up to see a squirrel or a Stellar's jay curiously watching us. We spotted coyotes on the edge of a meadow and along animal trails, moving quietly displaying curiosity with noses to the ground and ears perked up to catch sounds. Our observations triggered many discussions, and the children began to regard the animals as belonging in that habitat.

You do not need to live in a national park to be able to observe and become familiar with wildlife. Even in areas with dense human population, many forms of wildlife can be spotted or tracked. You can teach children to notice tracks in the snow or along a muddy shore. Examine *scat*, or feces, and search out evidence of browsing or grazing to reveal where animals have been eating. Most children have a natural curiosity about wild creatures and enjoy discovering these clues that help them learn more about animals' habitats.

Most wild animals go undetected. Insects inhabit a hidden world, often found beneath rocks and within rotting logs. Of the hundred million different species of animals now believed to exist on earth, most of them are insects! That is fortunate for us, because insects are vital for decomposition, pollination, and the food chain.

Birds rely on insects for their food; birds, too, are wild animals. Most of the birds children see in their backyard will never be touched by a human hand. Migrating birds might travel thousands of miles over perilous water bodies and through incredible weather conditions and end up right outside your window singing with the sunrise.

On walks through fields, look for mole tunnels as they crisscross your trail, listen for crickets chirping in the night, and search for salamanders under damp logs.

While animals are fascinating to study and draw, it is important to treat all living creatures with respect. If you catch any live animals to observe, always handle them as little as possible, and release them promptly, preferably where they were collected. Wild animals kept as pets rarely live for long, and the release of an animal teaches the children about the need to preserve intact habitats.

The investigations and activities in "Animal explorations" are designed to promote awareness of animals and their characteristics. Children will learn that all animals share certain features: mobility, sensory organs, and the ability to eat. "Microscope drawing" illustrates that a drop of pond water might be swarming with animals, each one tiny and complete. The spider's intricate weaving of threads might be better understood as the children weave their own threads on a branch in "Spider weaving." By drawing with a feather and noticing its light weight, a child will learn more about birds and flight. During this chapter's activities the children observe the wildlife which lives around them. The lessons they receive will be introduced by you but taught by the animals they observe.

1. What are the smallest animals?

Tiny animals and plants live in the soil, air, rivers, and oceans. Many are so small that they live in and on other animals. Some are even living on people, in your skin, hair, mouth, and within your nose and intestines! These tiny animals and plants are called *microbes*. Each microbe is made of one cell. A *cell* is the smallest unit of life. Even though microbes are just one cell, they carry on the same life functions as all living things: They take in food, water, and gases; get rid of waste material; change when the environment changes; and grow and make more of themselves.

The smallest animals are called *protozoa*. Protozoa look different from most other animals. If you use a microscope, you will see that they are often round with little hairs growing all around them, or they have whip-like tails that go back and forth. Protozoa are a food source for many little fish. The little

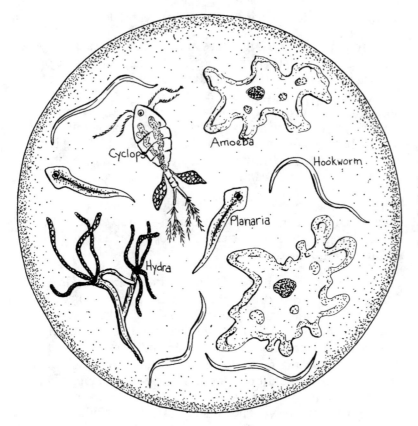

Labels in illustration: Cyclops, Amoeba, Hookworm, Planaria, Hydra

Microscopic animals share the characteristics that all animals possess: mobility, sensory organs, and the ability to eat.-

fish are eaten by larger fish, birds, and marine mammals. People also eat the larger fish. All of these larger animals depend on the tiny protozoa to supply them with a food source. Protozoa are essential in the food chain.

Protozoa can also be parasitic to all kinds of animals, including humans. An example is the *sporozoa*, which is a malaria parasite. If taken in by a mosquito and allowed to develop, that mosquito can transmit malaria to humans.

Most of the animals in the world are *invertebrates*, meaning that they have no backbone. All protozoa are invertebrates. Examples of other invertebrates are jellyfish, corals, worms, snails, crabs, lobsters, spiders, and all the insects. These invertebrates are not microscopic because they can be seen by the unaided human eye.

1. What are the smallest animals?   77

Research questions

Information to read aloud and research with your children:

A microscope works using lenses and light. A lens is usually a thin, circular glass, thicker in the middle, that bends rays of light so that when you look through it an object appears larger. A microscope uses several lenses. It also has a set of adjustments to give you control over how much you want to magnify. When you want to view something from a microscope, it must be small enough to fit on a glass slide. This slide is put on the stage over the mirror, and light is reflected through, so that the lenses inside can magnify the view for you.

With a microscope, you can easily explore the world of microbes. Prepare a *wet mount* by placing a drop of water in the center of a glass microscope slide. Gently lower a *cover slip* (at a 45° angle) onto the drop.

Prepare a wet mount using a drop of water from a pond. Examine your slide closely with the highest-power objective lens, and discover a variety of microbes. Make sketches of what you see. Compare the findings with wet mounts originating from water from melted snow, a mud puddle, and the kitchen sink. Make drawings of all the different slides and label them. To increase the amount of microbes, place some chopped up hay or wheat in the water. After a few days, a tremendous number of microbes will appear. Try different introduced substances, for example flowers, leaves, honey, and milk, to see what different microbes will appear. How did the pond water slide differ from the snow water slide? Why did the amount of microbes increase on the slide after adding the different food sources? What food source caused the greatest amount of increase? Why do you think this is so?

Microscope drawing

Indoor activity
Time needed: 30 minutes–1 hour
Materials needed:

- ❑ Microscope
- ❑ Viewing slides
- ❑ Material from nature
- ❑ Sketchbook/journal or large drawing paper
- ❑ Pencils
- ❑ Crayons, colored pencils, markers, or paint

1. On a walk, have the group collect decomposing vegetation, insect larva, or pond water to view later through a microscope.

2. After returning from the walk, the children should set the examples up on viewing slides or dishes and prepare to illustrate what is being viewed.

3. First, draw the specimens in small form in the sketchbooks or journals, and then label what they are and the magnification power used.

4. Next, do a second drawing using the same specimens, but the drawings should be as large as the entire sheet of paper.

5. Color in the shapes drawn. This second drawing is to be inspired from the drawing of the microbes, yet the children should be free to make abstract images.

6. Present the drawings and describe how microscopic images can develop into large abstract drawings.

2. What do bees & butterflies eat?

Bees gather and eat nectar and are some of the best pollinators in the world. They have long *probosces*, or feeding tubes, so they can reach deep into the flowers to gather nectar and spread pollen. Many wasps also take nectar from flowers. Wasps simply drink the nectar and do not transport pollen to their young as bees do. Because bees transport nectar to their young to eat, they are regularly carrying it, along with the pollen, and inadvertently depositing it in other flowers.

A group of flies known as the Syrphid flies, or hover flies, are harmless to people and are second only to bees as effective pollinators. These flies are brightly colored with orange, yellow, or red and black stripes, so that they closely resemble bees and wasps. They do not sting, however.

Butterflies eat nectar, and they fly constantly from plant to plant seeking it out. Although they have no interest in eating pollen, butterflies accidentally transport it and pollinate as they go. Moths are adapted to eat nectar from night bloomers with their long tongues, and they also inadvertently pollinate plants.

Bees gather pollen on their legs as they sip nectar from flowers.

The job of nectar-eating and pollination has not been left entirely to the insects, because other creatures enjoy sweets and have discovered the world of flowers. Some of these are hummingbirds, the tropical sunbirds, Australian birds called honeyeaters, many kinds of bats, the honey possum, bears, and several kinds of monkey-like lemurs and bush babies.

Research questions

Information to read aloud and research with your children:

Try to observe and make notes on as many nectar-feeding insects and birds as you can. Determine which plants were the most popular. Do the popular plants have certain colors or smells? Which sense do you think is the strongest for nectar eaters, their sense of smell or sight? How could you test to find out?

Bees are fascinating nectar feeders. With the African honeybee entering into the United States, many people are concerned how these "killer bees" will affect honeybees. Investigate what you can about these "killer bees." Why are they called that? How will they affect the other honeybees?

Drawing from a sweet picture collection

Indoor activity
Time needed: 30 minutes
Materials needed:

- ❑ Magazines that can be cut apart that include pictures of honey or nectar eaters
- ❑ Scissors
- ❑ Sketchbook/journal or drawing paper
- ❑ Pencils or markers

1. Have the group cut out pictures from magazines that include pictures of honey or nectar eaters, including insects, birds, and bats.

2. Next, each child should select a picture to draw from the assortment of cut-out pictures. Place the photograph under the paper and lightly trace it or draw light dots that can be connected to form the outline of the animals' shape.

3. Remove the picture from beneath the paper and study it closely while darkening or connecting the traced lines or dots. Then, complete the drawing of the animal's body. Finally, color the drawing.

4. Discuss how the animals' bodies are equipped to gather the nectar or honey.

5. Encourage the children to keep picture files of all different kinds of animals to be able to draw and study from later. Magazine pictures can be stored in file folders and filed alphabetically or by animal groups.

3. What are mollusks?

After insects, *mollusks* are the most diverse group of animals on earth. Most mollusks have bodies that are covered by a shell. Typical mollusks are snails, clams, and oysters. Slugs lack shells, but are also mollusks. Like other mollusks, slugs and snails have no bones. The soft slippery skin of both can dry out very easily because their skin is not waterproof. For this reason, slugs and snails produce a lot of slime to keep their skin moist. They also prefer to live in wet places. Both slugs and snails leave a slimy trail. They usually feed at night and hide under debris during the summer months.

Over 70,000 different kinds of snails and slugs are found in gardens, woods, fields, marshes, ponds, rivers, and oceans. Snails typically have a single coiled shell that can be rounded or flattened. Snails have a distinct head with a pair of sensory tentacles that can be extended or retracted. An eye is located at the base of each tentacle. Beneath the tentacles is the mouth, equipped with a rasping tongue that works back and forth like a file to shred food. Freshwater snails feed mostly on plants, although some eat dead animals. They are food themselves for many different kinds of fish and a few kinds of birds and animals. Snails and slugs crawl on a thick, muscular "foot" on the underside of their body.

Information to read aloud and research with your children:

Research questions

Observing land snails and slugs is best done on a drizzly night, early in the morning, following a heavy rain, or in generally wet places. Look for snails or slugs in the woods or gardens, under

leaves, stones, and rotting logs. If you live in a big city, check the parks, gardens, and window boxes. You can observe pond snails under pond weeds, floating plants, or submerged rocks. What do snails and slugs do in winter or when there is snow? Or when the weather is dry? Read about *estivation* in a book. Do snails and slugs estivate? What do snails and slugs eat? Are they scavengers? How do they locate their food? What are the effects of light and dark on snails and slugs?

Drawing a snail and slug hike

Outdoor activity
Time needed: 30 minutes
Materials needed:

- ❑ Sketchbook/journal or drawing paper
- ❑ Pencils
- ❑ Drawing boards
- ❑ Snails or slugs

1. Go for a snail and slug search on a damp day. Look around garden areas, under debris, and around ponds.
2. Each child should sit quietly and alone next to his or her found snail in its habitat for 15 minutes. Each should mark off a square foot around the snail or slug and begin to observe and draw it, without disturbing it.

Observing and drawing a small area helps children focus attention on insects and snails.

3. Let the children know that they can include in the drawing any other life that might crawl or buzz through the square foot area. Also, draw the leaves or grasses that the snail or slug is crawling on or include the soil's texture and color.

4. After 15 minutes, everyone should gather together and show the drawings and discuss any discoveries made about the snails and slugs.

4. Do earthworms eat soil?

Earthworms do eat soil and pass it out through their bodies. The tunnels that are created while earthworms are eating allow air into the soil; this process is called *aeration* and improves the soil as it turns it over. Earthworm tunnels also allow rainwater to percolate deep into the soil. Worms also eat leaves, leaving small piles of castings behind them.

Earthworms are *hermaphrodite*, which means that they are each equipped with both male and female parts. They cannot fertilize themselves, though, so they do mate with one another. If you see two worms laying side by side, they are probably mating.

Worms like dark, moist places. A good time to see earthworms is early in the morning after a rain. Earthworms have segmented bodies that move with the help of tiny backward-facing hairs called *setae*. These hairs help secure the worm as it moves part of its body forward. If you have seen a bird trying to pull an earthworm from its burrow, you know that the setae will help the worm put up a good fight to hang on to the ground.

Information to read aloud and research with your children:

Research questions

Using a tall, thin glass, collect different colors of moist soils and put them in distinct layers in the glass. Collect several worms after a rain and put them in your soil-filled glass. Add leaves on top of the soil. Put a light piece of gauze over the top of the glass and secure it with a rubber band. Put black construction paper around the glass and set it in a quiet dark place for a day or two. Check it after the time has passed by removing the black paper. Note how the earthworms have mixed up the soil layers and moved them around. Perhaps when you check your glass you will see an earthworm digging right along the side of the glass. Can you see the segments of its body? Can you tell which end contains its mouth? What happens when you leave

the paper off the glass for a few minutes? Release your earthworms in a moist garden in the evening when you are done observing them.

Trapping and drawing soil creatures

Outdoor activity
Time needed: Overnight plus 15 minutes of drawing time
Materials needed:

- ❑ Sketchbook/journal
- ❑ Pencils
- ❑ Spoon for digging
- ❑ Empty yogurt or other plastic container
- ❑ Piece of apple
- ❑ Rocks

1. Have the children dig a hole about five inches deep into a moist soil. Place an empty plastic container in the hole with a piece of fruit for bait.

2. Set little rocks around the top of the hole with a larger rock balanced on top of it. The rocks will help keep the container in the shade and keep predators out.

3. In the morning, see what has fallen into the trap. Observe and note if it is a worm, earwig, centipede, or pillbug. Do some quick sketches of the soil creatures, then release them in a shaded place where they can scurry under a rock. Observe your sketches and research to find out more information about the invertebrates that you captured.

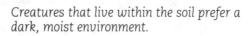

Creatures that live within the soil prefer a dark, moist environment.

First of all, not all spiders weave webs. Some are hunters that do not depend on webs to catch their food. A few spiders can be poisonous, so be sure to check which ones are native to your area and be able to identify and avoid any potentially dangerous spiders. Some spiders live in the ground or in logs. For the many spiders that do use webs, however, the web is an incredible food trap.

A spider has three tubes located at the end of its abdomen, connected to glands within the abdomen. By holding these three tubes together, the spider weaves a thick silk thread, or the spider can weave thin separate threads by leaving them apart. The spider's tubes, or *spinnerets*, are pressed against an object, and then the spider forces out some of the liquid silk. As the spider moves, more silk is emitted behind it, and the liquid hardens in the air. When the thread is hardened, the spider climbs back up the thread, beginning a second thread. It continues until it forms a figure like the spokes of a wheel. This spoked wheel is connected with a concentric pattern that the spider begins from the center of the web, working slowly outward and around.

Because the spider coats its legs with an oily substance from its mouth, it can travel around on its web without being caught. In a radial web, the spokes are not sticky, only the circular strands are; the spiders get around most of the time on the nonsticky spokes.

Information to read aloud and research with your children:

Research questions

Spiders are common in many habitats. They even have been found living in silken säcs underwater and have been seen hanging from the cliffs off high mountain peaks. You probably have heard that spider silk is stronger than steel. Can you design an experiment to find out if that is true?

Webs are easy to find in your house. Look for them in corners that are hard to reach, such as near the hot-water heater or in your garage. Find a web with a spider. Identify the spider to make sure it doesn't bite or sting. Avoid touching the spider, or wear gloves as you coax the spider off the web without hurting it. Take a sheet of black construction paper and lift the web gently, it will stick to your paper. Examine the web with a

Spiders do not become entangled in their own webs because they step only on the dry spokes and not on the sticky spiral lines.

magnifying glass for its amazing construction, the food that is caught in it, and the size. See if the spider has constructed a new web a day or two later in the same place where you took down the first one. Predict and keep track of what the spider is catching to eat. How long do you think spiders live?

86 Animal explorations

Indoor or outdoor activity
Time needed: 30 minutes
Materials needed:

- ❑ Thin forked tree branch
- ❑ Yarn
- ❑ Scissors

1. Each child should find a forked tree branch that is a total of two to three feet long. Find the branches on the ground; don't break off live branches from trees.

2. Have each child tie one piece of yarn to one of the fork's ends, and bring it across and wrap the yarn around the other fork end. Return this piece of yarn back to the first fork end and tie it again. Snip the yarn. You should now have a double string running between the forked branch.

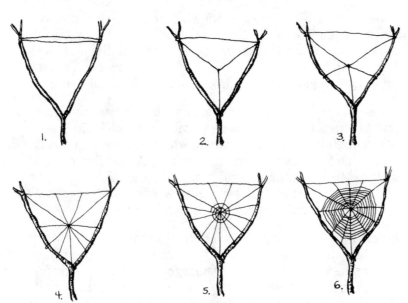

Making a spider web from yarn or string allows the children to better understand the pattern used in an orb web.

3. Have each child take another piece of yarn and tie it to the lower of the double strings and tie the other end of it to where the two forks meet on the branch. Snip the yarn. They now have formed the center point for the web.

5. How do spiders make a web?   87

4. Next, have them tie several strings from different places on the branch to the center knot, to form radial-like spokes on a wheel.

5. Each child should now cut a piece of yarn about four feet long. Roll it up to handle it easily. Take the end of this long piece and tie it on a spoke close to the center of the web. Take this piece and begin to work clockwise around the web, encircling each spoke that they come to before proceeding to the next spoke. Tie the yarn to every three or four spokes they encircle to keep it from slipping.

6. Finally, after the yarn has been woven around the web five or six rotations, tie the yarn tightly when the web is finished. Compare the childrens' webs with the spider's.

6. Where do frogs go during the winter?

Frogs disappear for many months of the year by hibernating down in the mud at the bottom of their ponds or on land beneath the frost line. When they hibernate, their bodies go into a dormant state, with very slow heartbeats, using as little energy as possible. Like other cold-blooded reptiles and amphibians, they cannot generate their own heat and must hibernate, or slow their metabolic rate, or they will freeze.

When it gets warm in the spring and summer, you can hear and see frogs near ponds as they emerge and call for a mate. Males do most of the vocalization, while females are usually quiet. The females are attracted to the special call of her species. Although male frogs do mount females during mating, their eggs are fertilized when the female drops her eggs in the water and the male releases his sperm over them.

Frogs' eggs hatch, forming tiny tadpoles that live in the water. Very few tadpoles live to maturity because many predators and environmental factors work against them. Predaceous diving beetles, crayfish, and dragonfly nymphs eat them heartily. If the tadpoles' pools dry up, the tadpoles will not survive. Also, tadpoles have been found to be sensitive to acid rain.

If the tadpoles survive, their legs eventually emerge and their tails are absorbed, resulting in them developing into a mature frog. Once mature, they will primarily eat insects, catching them with their long sticky tongues.

Information to read aloud and research with your children:

How do frogs breathe during their many months buried beneath the mud of a pond? Why do you think frogs lay sometimes thousands of eggs at a time? How many of these thousand eggs eventually become frogs? During the spring, make regular visits to a pond and record when the male frogs start making their calls. Note when you first start seeing tadpoles along the edge of the pond. Estimate how long it will take for the tadpoles to become adults. Begin to make regular observations and see if your estimate was close. The process of changing from an egg to a tadpole to a frog is called a *metamorphosis*. Can you think of any other animals that go through a metamorphosis?

Observing a tadpole change into a frog offers the children the opportunity to witness a metamorphosis.

Outdoor or indoor activity
Time needed: 1 hour
Materials needed:

Frog potato prints

- ❑ Large potatoes
- ❑ Pencils

6. Where do frogs go during the winter?   89

❑ Sharp knives
❑ Tempera paint
❑ Paintbrushes
❑ Drawing paper

1. After a talk about frogs and their stages of metamorphosis, let the children know that they will each make three potato prints to represent the eggs, the tadpole, and the adult frog.

2. Use caution as this activity requires the use of a sharp knife to cut the potato print. Each child should cut two cleaned potatoes in half. Allow them to dry for a few minutes, while the child sketches the drawings of the three stages of a frog's life.

3. The sketches on paper should be the same size as the smooth side of the potato halves. The drawings should use simple shapes. Redraw the sketches lightly on the potato with the pencil. Cut around the drawn shapes, leaving them in relief. (The extra potato half can be used for another design or if the child wants to redo one of these designs.)

4. Using the tempera paint and brush, paint thickly on the potato design, but keep the paint on the relief part of the design. Then print the frog designs by turning the potato over and pressing it firmly on the paper. Make the three designs in order to reflect the metamorphosis of the frog.

7. How do feathers help birds?

All birds—and only birds—have feathers. Birds are able to fly largely because of their feathers, powerful wings, and hollow bones. These characteristics couple high power with low weight, allowing the bird to fly.

The insulating, waterproof layer of a bird's body is made up of the feathers, known as its *plumage*. Each feather is a light structure made of a fibrous substance called *keratin*. Each feather has a central shaft with thin filaments called *barbs*. Like body hairs, feathers have nerve endings attached to them, as well as muscles that can fluff them up to conserve heat. The tiny pits in a bird's skin are called *feather follicles*. Each one has a feather in it, just like the hair follicles found on human skin. The two main jobs of feathers are heat conservation and flight. Oily feathers give buoyancy to water fowl by increasing their volume while increasing their weight only slightly.

*The functions of feathers
are flight, warmth,
and camouflage.*

Feathers serve birds as functions of flight, warmth, and as color
markings. The feathers might serve to camouflage the bird, for
reproductive strategies, or as recognition marks. Many small
perching birds blend in with their surroundings to avoid contact

7. How do feathers help birds?   91

with their predators. Brilliantly colored throat patches or the striking colors of many males attract the female to promote a sexual interaction. *Recognition marks*, such as the white flash on a junko's feathers, only seen when in flight, warn other junkos that danger might be near.

Usually after the breeding season, the worn-out feathers of birds are lost or *molted*. Within a gradual period of several weeks to months, the feathers grow back. Birds have more feathers in the winter than in the summer in order to keep warm.

Research questions

Information to read aloud and research with your children:

Every winter, when temperatures drop in northern latitudes, billions of birds migrate south to warmer climates. And every spring, when temperatures rise up north, these same birds fly north to their breeding grounds, sometimes returning to within half a mile of where they were born.

Depending on where you live, you should be able to observe bird migrations. Keep track of migration activities in early spring and again in early autumn. Note dates of arrival and departure. The best time of day to do your observing is in the early morning. Do arriving birds fly singularly or in groups? Are both sexes around at the same time in the spring? Research where the birds that are in your area go during the winter months. Do some birds come to your area for winter?

Using feathers as drawing tools

Indoor or outdoor activity
Time needed: 30 minutes
Materials needed:

- ❏ Feathers
- ❏ Knife
- ❏ Beets (or tempera paints or bottled inks)
- ❏ Sketchbook/journal or drawing paper

1. Boil and simmer the beets. Remove the juice and let it cool, to be used for drawing inks.

2. Have the children collect the feathers either from a farm, from the woods, or from someone's collection, and carefully sharpen their ends with knives. Discuss the feathers' structure and their weight.

3. Using the feather pen and beet ink, each child can draw a picture of the bird where the feather originated. Also, they can draw the beets, where the ink originated.

4. It is fun to practice writing letters with the feathered pen and inks, and discuss how earlier people used these types of tools.

8. Why do animals have whiskers?

Most animals who have whiskers use them as sensory detectors. The whiskers help them figure out their location. On most mammals, whiskers are as wide as the widest part of their body. This width enables the animal to stick its head in a hole and figure out if its whole body can get through that hole. If its whiskers are pushed back, the animal will retreat, knowing the rest of its body wouldn't make it through.

The whiskers of the marmot help it to explore its rocky habitat.

Insect-eating birds have whiskers. These whiskers, called *rictal bristles*, are used to help scoop up insects while the bird is in flight. Swifts, swallows, and whippoorwills are three different birds with rictal bristles.

Fish have whiskers that are tactile; they help them to be more aware of their surroundings. Like fish, burrowing insects use their whiskers to help explore their surroundings.

On humans, men generally have whiskers on their faces. These whiskers, if allowed to grow, keep the face warmer in cold temperatures. Most women don't have much facial hair, but compared to men, women do have an extra layer of fatty tissue that helps them remain warm in cold climates.

Research questions

Information to read aloud and research with your children:

What animals can you think of that have whiskers that live in your area? Rabbits, deer, squirrels, dogs, cats, mice, ... In fact, most mammals do have whiskers. Are whiskers made of exactly the same materials that hair or fur is made up of? If so, why are they so sensitive to their surroundings? Have you ever seen fish with whiskers? Examine dead insects with your magnifying glass to see if they have whiskers also. What do humans use instead of whiskers to sense our environment?

Paper mash whisker masks

Indoor activity
Time needed: Three different 1-hour periods
Materials needed:

- ❑ Large round balloons
- ❑ Newspaper
- ❑ Glue
- ❑ Water
- ❑ Tempera paint
- ❑ Yarn
- ❑ Varnish
- ❑ Scissors

Mask-making provides a creative way to study animal faces and the use of whiskers.

1. After you talk about all the different animals that have a form of whiskers, have each child make a mask from their choice of a whiskered animal. Before each 1-hour period, have a mask completed as far as the children should get that day, to demonstrate.

2. The water-glue mixture is one part glue to three parts water. Have it mixed in one bowl for every three children.

3. Have the children tear many strips of newsprint (1×6 inches) and soak them in the glue mixture. Have them blow up their balloons; each balloon should be large enough to cover the child's face.

4. Work with one strip at a time. Remove the excess water from the strip by running your fingers down the strip. Lay each piece of strained newsprint over one side of the balloon surface. Laying them in random directions of several layers will make the balloon stronger. Allow the balloons to dry; it will take several days. Store them

8. Why do animals have whiskers?   95

carefully. Have the children put their names on their balloons.

5. The second session will be to build the features on the mask. Remake the glue mixture as before, but cut the newsprint in smaller pieces and soak it longer.

6. With this mash mixture of newsprint build features such as ears, snouts, and cheeks. Lay longer strips (1×6 inches) over the mash to hold the features in place. Again allow several days to dry.

7. In the third session, the children can paint, add yarn, and varnish their masks. Use broom straws or yarn for whiskers. Tempera paint dries quickly; the varnish is the final coat over the paint. Finally, the unworked back of the mask should be cut away, the balloon should be removed, eye holes should be cut, and a string should be attached to tie them on the back of the children's heads.

9. Why do some animals have hooves & some have paws?

Most animals with paws and claws are carnivores. *Carnivores* are hunters, and they are dependent on the ability to stalk quietly to capture prey. Examples of animals with paws and claws are the cat family, bears, raccoons, and coyotes. Many of the pawed animals are known for their ability to climb, and their ability to manipulate their paws as if they had a thumb similar to humans. Cats are known to be able to open doors, bears will get into picnic baskets, and raccoons will hold their prey near the stream. None of these animals' paws have quite the dexterity of the human hand, but combined with their mouths and perseverance, they are able to use their paws to open and hold things. Some clawed animals use different strategies in stalking their prey. Cats don't show their claws except when using them, while those in the dog family always have their claws exposed. Dogs use traction and speed for their hunting, while cats use stealth and quietness to catch their food.

Those animals with hooves are *herbivores*. They graze on various plants in their habitat. These hooves are used to break

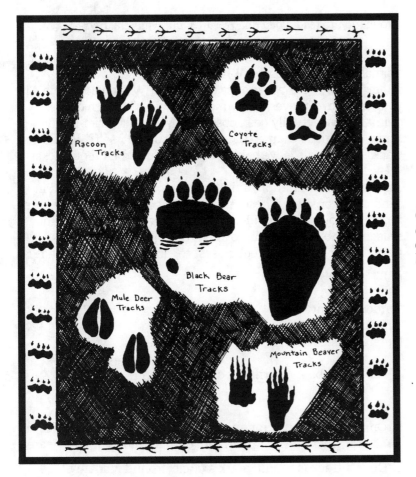

Observing and drawing animal tracks helps give clues about the animals that live in the habitat.

through ground surfaces, for balance, and for defense. Examples of animals with hooves are deer, sheep, horses, and elk. Hoofed animals are known for speed, grace, and in some cases climbing abilities. Mountain sheep and mountain goats have some of the greatest known climbing abilities for a large mammal; they can climb onto ledges where wolves and bears cannot follow them.

9. Why do some animals have hooves & some have paws?   97

Research questions

Information to read aloud and research with your children:

Make a list of animals that have paws and make another list of animals that have hooves. What are the different survival strategies for these two groups of animals? What wild animals in your area have hooves, and which have paws? Which of these animals have actually been observed? Why is it easier to find tracks of animals than actually see the animal itself? What other tracks do animals leave behind them, besides their foot tracks?

After close examination, animal tracks can often be found in sand, mud, or snow. These tracks make good investigative clues for you to follow and to identify. An animal's size, speed, and seasonal habits can be discovered through the study of its tracks. Which are your feet closest to, hooves or paws? What is your strategy for survival?

Drawing animal tracks

Outdoor activity
Time needed: Open
Materials needed:

❑ Sketchbook/journal or drawing paper
❑ Pencils

1. On an outing, hunt for animal tracks. The best place to find animal tracks is along a stream or in a muddy or snowy area.

2. Once a track is found, mark a circle around it so it will be easy to see. Try to draw the tracks with your fingers in the dirt or snow. Note if they are of a hoofed animal or one with paws.

3. Sketch any observed tracks. The drawings are done to keep a record of the animals found in that location and so the children can identify the tracks for themselves in the future.

10. Why do animals have differently shaped teeth?

Herbivores (grazers) such as deer and sheep have large flat molars with complex ridges and cusps. Plant eaters have good grinding and chewing teeth because they must be able to break down the cell wall or the *cellulose* that the plant cells are enclosed in. Cellulose cannot be digested, so animals must be

able to chew right through it to get to the foodstuffs. This is why a cow, deer, or any grazer is known to "chew its cud" for long periods of time as it breaks down the cellulose.

Carnivorous (meat-eating) animals have more pointed teeth than herbivores. Their teeth are better adapted for cutting and shredding than for grinding. Carnivores need not chew their food so laboriously. There are no protective cells in meat, and consequently, carnivores often gulp their food, rarely chewing it at all.

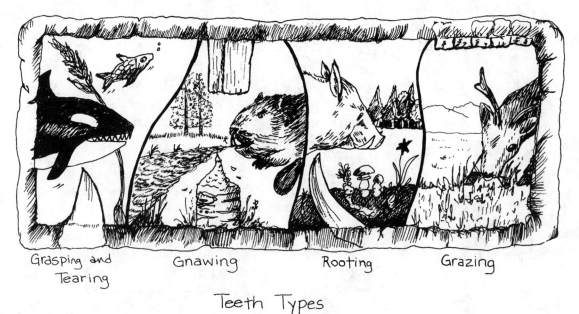

Grasping and Tearing   Gnawing   Rooting   Grazing

Teeth Types

In the animal kingdom, teeth perform different functions.

Animals that are omnivores (eat both meat and plants), such as bears and people, have both the flat grinding teeth along with the sharp canine teeth used to rip and tear.

The teeth of snakes are thin and sharp. Snake teeth usually curve backwards and are used to capture prey, not to break it down. Snakes generally swallow their prey whole.

10. Why do animals have differently shaped teeth? 99

Research questions   *Information to read aloud and research with your children:*

Try to imagine cutting raw meat with just your teeth or chomping mouthful after mouthful of dried hay. Different animals have adapted different teeth systems to eat their food. As you are observing wildlife, try to imagine what kind of teeth they must have. For example, could you tell the difference in the skulls of a squirrel, coyote, deer, and mouse by studying their mouths and teeth? What could you learn about different animals by keeping a skull collection?

Pen and ink skull drawings   Indoor or outdoor activity
Time needed: 30 minutes–1 hour
Materials needed:

- ❏ Clean animal skull
- ❏ Sketchbook/journal or drawing paper
- ❏ Black piece of construction paper or black cloth
- ❏ Pencils, pen and ink, or black markers
- ❏ Black poster board or mat board

1. Place the found animal skull on a piece of black construction paper or black cloth in order to see it better.

2. Determine what animal the skull came from by noting its teeth, its size, and its shape.

3. Using a pencil, the children can draw the outline of the skull. Encourage them to include as many details as possible through close observation.

4. Next, have them go over the pencil lines with ink or black markers to clearly define the skull. Try to include every little curve and detail. Blacken in the skulls eyes and nasal cavity to increase the contrast of the drawing.

5. Finally, have the children carefully measure and cut a piece of black poster board or mat board to form a frame for the skull drawings. Mount and hang them to educate others about the skulls you have observed.

All animals do show some sensitivity or response to either light and/or sound vibrations. While we humans have a high overall level of sensory development, our individual senses are not nearly as developed compared to some other animal species. For example, the olfactory sense of bears or the vision of hawks is much greater than our sense of smell or sight.

Fish and amphibians, two kinds of animals that spend most of their lives in water, have two water-filled tubes lying along each side of the body just under the skin. These are called *lateral lines*. They enable the animals to detect water currents and pressure changes, and the animals use this information to find their way around.

Few insects have hearing organs located on their heads. Instead, their ears, or *tympanic* organs, are located in various parts of their bodies. In the grasshopper and cricket, the tympanic organs are found on the tibia of each foreleg. In the cicada, they are found on the bottom of the abdomen. Moths' tympanic organs are located on either side of the rear of the thorax or the front part of the abdomen. This thin membrane vibrates when sound waves strike it, and the vibrations are passed on to the auditory nerve. Through the auditory nerve, sound is detected within the brain. Most insects have tiny hairs that react to sound vibrations in the air. Sometimes these hairs are found on the antennae, and some are all over the body, as in some caterpillars.

Most insects have two forms of vision, a pair of large compound eyes and a number of small, simple eyes or *ocelli*. The ocelli act to distinguish light from dark. The compound eye is responsible for perceiving a degree of form perception, depth perception, and color awareness. Most caterpillars only have ocelli, and therefore their vision is minimal, seeing one or two inches in front of them. Insects cannot focus their vision, and distant objects are blurred. Since, at a distance, moving objects are easier to detect, remaining still keeps a wasp or bee from coming close and stinging.

Research questions

Information to read aloud and research with your children:

Many insects, for example, moths and beetles, are very attracted to light sources. In the summer months, hang a white sheet outside near the edge of a wooded area or a fence row in your backyard. Run out a light bulb on an extension cord from the house and shine it directly onto the sheet. Investigate your collection at all hours of the night to see what you have attracted. Are there many moths and beetles with different colors and sizes? Keep your sheet up for several nights. Did you collect more insects during different times of the night? Try different colored lights on the sheet to see if it makes any difference about collecting insects. Make sketches of your insects before they fly away.

Moths can be lured in with lights at night so that they can be observed and drawn.

Outdoor activity
Time needed: 30 minutes
Materials needed:

- ❑ White sheet
- ❑ Light source
- ❑ Extension cord
- ❑ Containers (jars; some with holes in the lids)
- ❑ Sketchbook/journal or drawing paper
- ❑ Pencils and markers
- ❑ Drawing boards

1. Catching insects on a sheet at night is described in the research questions on page 102. Studying and drawing night insects can be a fascinating way to learn more about their structure and how they use their senses. These animals can be studied without being handled. If you do touch them to look at their undersides or wing patterns, do it gently. Always release the animals when you are done drawing and studying them.

2. While beetles can be transferred to a jar for study, moths should not be kept in a jar because they might damage themselves on the glass walls. Observe and study the moths as they lie on the sheet.

3. Use field guides and library books to determine how they hear, see, and smell.

12. Why are some animals camouflaged?

Early people often camouflaged themselves by wrapping buffalo robes around themselves while hunting game. They needed to blend into the landscape to be successful in their hunting. *Camouflage* is blending into the landscape in order to survive. Concealment or camouflage is found at all levels of the animal kingdom. An example of background matching is found with fish eggs that exist in the open sea; these eggs, often completely transparent, are all but invisible to the eye.

Camouflage is important because most animals have competition between species for food and shelter. This competition is often between each species and its natural enemies. Many animals depend on their color, shape, or ability to mimic to defend themselves or be able to sneak up on their prey.

Lines, spots, and stripes on animals are called *disruptive* patterns, and these patterns conceal many different species. Think of the brown and gray spotted plumage of many female birds, adapted for sitting quietly on eggs in the nest. The ability to stay still is very important in understanding camouflage. For many animals, their camouflage and the ability to stay still are their only defenses against predators. In some species, the camouflaged nest of the animal must protect the eggs.

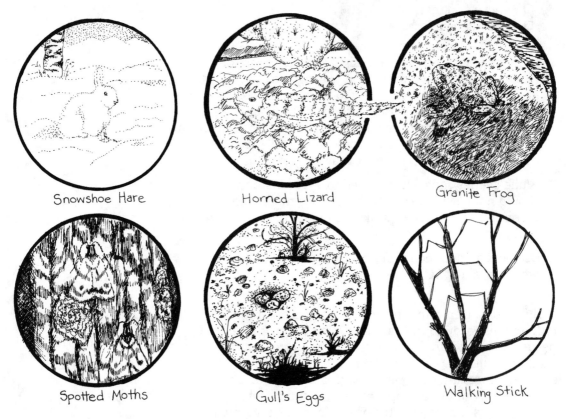

Snowshoe Hare   Horned Lizard   Granite Frog

Spotted Moths   Gull's Eggs   Walking Stick

Many animal species have adapted different camouflage strategies to avoid being captured.

Some animals' camouflage doesn't always conceal, but instead it gives off false information. *Mimicry*, or the copying of the shape, color, and habits of an offensive or disgusting species by other animals, is a very effective form of camouflage. For example, a very delicious butterfly, the viceroy, is colored the

same as, or mimics, the monarch butterfly, which is not very tasty to birds. Birds, therefore, often won't eat the viceroy because they mistake it for the bad-tasting monarch. In every case, mimics only copy animals that bite, sting, or give off bitter secretions.

Information to read aloud and research with your children:

Research questions

What happens when an animal that is perfectly camouflaged to hide in its habitat is forced out of its habitat or that habitat is destroyed? Zebras and giraffes are examples of animals that were once forest dwellers and their size and coloration are still indicative of that. Now they live on the African open grasslands and their coloration and size does not offer any protective disguise. Research, and if possible, conduct an investigation on what happens to animals that are adapted to certain habitats when their habitat is altered or destroyed. Where would examples of destroyed habitat be found today?

Drawing animal disguises

Outdoor activity
Time needed: 1 hour
Materials needed:

- ❏ Sketchbook/journal or paper
- ❏ Pencils or markers
- ❏ Drawing boards

1. Before going out for a walk, discuss animal patterns and coloration used for camouflage. Define symmetry as shapes or position of parts that are the same, yet on opposite sides of a dividing line. Give an example of a butterfly's wings pattern as being symmetrical. Ask for other examples.

2. Look for and draw all the different examples of patterns and camouflage that can be discovered on a walk. Note the repeating shapes found in frog's eggs, the symmetry found in a feather, the design of a snail's shell, or the pattern on a bumblebee's body.

3. Each illustration should be labeled as to where it was found and the date. Keep a tally of how many different patterns and examples of camouflage that have been found.

4. Discuss which elements of camouflage and use of patterns that were found to be the most interesting. How would they be effective to conceal the animal?

13. Can some animals change their disguises?

Some animals are known for their ability to change color to camouflage only in a stressful situation. Many frogs and toads are able to change color to conform with their surroundings. Their permanent markings contain pigments that can darken or lighten their bodies in response to changes in temperatures, touch, or moisture. In the ocean, a species of fish called flatfish or flounder have the ability to change color rapidly to harmonize with different backgrounds. This color change is the result of the amount of light received by the eye and by light-sensitive organs in the skin. The octopus can also make quick color changes by expanding or contracting its pigment cells, which release shades of blue, brown, green, orange, or brown.

Some animals actually digest or put on the colors of their host, which makes their appearance blend in with their surroundings to avoid capture. A slow-moving sea slug, the *nudibranch*, actually ingests portions of its home, living coral. The brilliant colors of the coral show through the nudibranch, allowing it to match perfectly with its host, affording good protection from other predators.

Some camouflage is related to seasonal changes. Many small mammals adapt a lighter fur coloration during the winter snows. Some animals that change colors with the seasons are hares, weasels, and ptarmigans.

Most insects cannot make instantaneous color changes because they lack the cells that control the movement of pigment. The process of changing colors for them involves *molting*, or the growing of a new skin, which takes time. However, insects are the most specialized when it comes to coloration in the blending with their permanent surroundings. Most of their colors come from the colors of the food that they eat; therefore they blend in with their surroundings.

Often adult mammals are disguised by one color scheme, and their babies by another. The babies are usually mottled, while the adults are usually a solid color. A strong contrasting color change for mammals is demonstrated by the seals of the North Atlantic. An adult has a sleek gray or black pelt, while the babies blend in perfectly with the white frozen snow pack.

Research questions

Information to read aloud and research with your children:

Consider why certain animals are colored, patterned, or shaped the way that they are. Try to think of an interesting example of a mammal, reptile, fish, bird, amphibian, and insect, and be able to explain why they appear the way they do. What does breeding and mating have to do with the way the animal appears?

Hidden animal drawing

Indoor activity
Time needed: 1 hour
Materials needed:

- ❏ Sketchbook/journal
- ❏ Drawing paper
- ❏ Pencils
- ❏ Markers
- ❏ Books for research

These children are discussing the best way to hide camouflaged animals in their vegetation.

13. Can some animals change their disguises?   107

1. Discuss all the different camouflage methods used by animals. Refer to the notes made in the sketchbooks or journals from the previous activity on looking for animal disguises.

2. Have the children each create an imaginary drawing of hidden animals that are highly camouflaged in their surroundings. Include the appropriate vegetation for the animal's surroundings in the drawings.

3. Encourage the children to use examples of animal camouflage that they have personally witnessed. Also, use library books or books from home that show examples of camouflage for ideas.

4. Display the drawings. See if friends and family can find the hidden, camouflaged animals.

14. What kinds of shelters do animals build?

Birds build nests for themselves as a part of their reproductive process. Most songbirds construct their nests in two phases. First, the bowl shape is made in the tree with grasses and twigs; second, the nest is cushioned with added feathers. Nests are made to be comfortable for the female, as she loses many of her feathers on her underside; this is called the *brooding patch*. This bare piece of skin is sent an increased amount of blood to enable the mother to keep her eggs warm and is very sensitive to feeling. The added feathers cushion her brooding patch.

Rodents build tunnels for shelter. The soil composition is a factor determining where they can make their tunnels. The soil cannot be too loose or sandy or the tunnels will collapse. The tunnels are for sleeping, searching for food, and escaping predators. Usually the sleeping tunnel is located beneath a boulder or a bush, giving it extra protection against any invaders.

Many of the larger mammals—such as mountain lions, coyotes, and bears—have an established den used mainly when the female is raising her young. She might choose a shallow cave, a jumble of fallen logs, or thick brush to hide in. The males rarely spend very much time in the den. Bears enter their deep sleep in a similar hideout.

Bees build beehives. The worker bees actually construct the hive from beeswax, which they form by a special process of converting honey to a waxy substance. As many as 20,000–40,000 bees in an individual hive live and work together.

Information to read aloud and research with your children:

Have you ever built a shelter before? Perhaps it was a tree house, a lean-to made from branches and a rain poncho, or maybe it was a hut made out of mud and sticks. When you spent time inside a shelter you built yourself, did you feel that your imagination was extra active? Why do you think that the shelter triggered your imagination?

Did your shelter help to protect you in any way? How do shelters made by wild animals help to protect them? Have you ever thought about how difficult it would be to build a bird's nest with just your mouth and feet? Birds primarily use their beaks and feet to assemble the materials, weave little stems, leaves, and feathers, and build their nests. Try an investigation to build a shelter with your hands tied behind your back and see how well it turns out.

Outdoor activity
Time needed: 2–3 hours
Materials needed:

- ❏ Shovels
- ❏ Waterproof clothing
- ❏ Snow

1. After you talk about shelters that animals make, encourage the children to make a shelter of their own. It's best to have three or four children working on a snow shelter. For a larger group, build several snow shelters.
2. Have the children work where the snow drifts are already built up into mounds. If there are no drifts, make one by shoveling together snow in a pile at least 8 hours before the group is ready to dig, as the pile needs to "set" before being dug into. (It can also be piled up a day or two in advance of the snow-shelter digging.)

14. What kinds of shelters do animals build?   109

3. Have the children take turns shoveling out the snow. An entrance tunnel is dug first, 2 to 4 feet long, and only dug high enough for their bodies to be able to slip through.

4. After shoveling and removing the snow from the tunnel, begin to dig the cave itself. The roof needs to stay curved, and the ceiling thickness should remain consistent for strong support. You can test the thickness with a stick or pole; it should be around 12 inches thick.

5. Digging the shelter floor a foot higher than the entrance tunnel's mouth will make it warmer, because the cave chamber is out of a draft. The ceiling should be rubbed smooth with gloved or mittened hands to alleviate dripping.

It takes a great deal of work and group cooperation to make a snow shelter.

15. Do animals have a memory?

It used to be generally believed that humans used intelligence and animals used instinct for survival. Now we understand that many animals do learn much of their behavior, as well as being born with a genetic ability to perform certain acts. Just as with small children, many animals, from a tiny chick to young turtles, rely on environmental reinforcements to learn to survive. Sensitivity to hot and cold teaches them where to sleep

to stay alive, available food sources teach the young where they can eat to survive, and parental coaching trains young wildlife how to survive predator attacks and where to go for an assured food supply.

Bees demonstrate an amazing ability to remember where they found a food source. They memorize the route after feeding and return to the hive to do a "dance" for the other bees to teach them the source of the nectar. The other worker bees gather around the dancer, touching her with their antennae so they can sense her direction and the number of times she vibrates. They then leave the hive and fly almost directly to the nectar source. While the dance and the ability to decipher it apparently is instinctual, the worker bee does rely on her memory to remember the key information to include in the dance.

Information to read aloud and research with your children:

Research questions

How can a pet animal be tested for its memory? Brainstorm how to devise a humane experiment using your own pet or teaming up with a small group to share an animal for the experiment. Some ideas for testing methods could be to devise a maze with a food source, verbal directions, or hiding an animal toy in the same place to see if the pet knows to return to find it. A variety of pets, such as dogs, cats, mice, rats, gerbils, fish, turtles, and birds can be tested and compared for their memory abilities.

Outdoor or indoor activity
Time needed: 30 minutes
Materials needed:

Testing our drawing memory

- ❏ Sketchbook/journal or paper
- ❏ Pencils
- ❏ Objects from nature
- ❏ Drawing boards

1. Have the children gather objects from nature and compose a still life. The group can sit in a circle around the still life.

2. Everyone should study the still life for 1 minute silently, without drawing.

3. Next, turn around after 1 minute and face away from the still life. Draw it from memory, without turning around, for two minutes.

4. After two minutes give a signal for the group to turn to face the still life again and silently study it for another 1 minute. Usually individuals will be more clearly "seeing" the still life this second viewing.

5. Again, signal to turn away from the still life and resume drawing for another 2 minutes.

Children's awareness of what is around them is developed when they do memory drawings.

112   *Animal explorations*

6. Signal to turn for the final time toward the still life, and, with the drawings at hand, tell the group to finish any details of the still life. Encourage them to not erase, instead, work with "mistakes" rather than starting over. Draw lines over lines, shapes over shapes, if necessary; this will add interest to the drawing.

7. Discuss how it felt to rely on memory to try to do a drawing. What was the biggest challenge of this activity?

16. How smart are animals?

The animals known to be the most intelligent are often those that live the longest. Parrots and jays live much longer than many other birds, and they are considered some of the smartest in their communication abilities. Dolphins can live for 35 years or more, and elephants can survive until 60 or older. On the other hand, animals that live brief lives are not thought of as great learners, but rather as animals whose behavior is patterned in their genes. For example, a fly lives such a short time that they don't have time to learn how to make a shelter or be taught how to care for their young. Therefore, it is programmed into them upon birth.

Many people are beginning to change their minds about whether animals can "think" or not. For a long time, humans were declared to be the only ones able to have intelligence, allowing us to feel superior to the rest of the animal kingdom. But, in fact, now it is known that many animals have high levels of intelligence. Many birds, dogs, monkeys, dolphins, and others have proven levels of intelligence studied by scientists recently. Rather than us feeling superior, we can now feel more connected to the rest of the animal world. It is exciting to learn about the studies where people have learned to communicate with gorillas, dolphins, and other highly intelligent animals. Perhaps we can understand our own true nature better by learning about and respecting other animal life on the planet.

Information to read aloud and research with your children:

Research questions

How much can we find out about animal intelligence? What sign of intelligence do you think is the most important: language, memory, or use of tools? Does the size of the brain influence the level of intelligence of an animal? Are there ways that human intelligence really differs from that of the other animals on earth? Create an investigation to solve one of these questions.

16. How smart are animals? 113

Drawing the smartest animal you know

Indoor or outdoor activity
Time needed: 30 minutes–1 hour
Materials needed:

- ❏ Sketchbook/journal or paper
- ❏ Pencils or markers
- ❏ Drawing boards
- ❏ Intelligent animal

1. Discuss what animals the children feel are very smart and discuss indicators of intelligence. The children will study and draw from a live animal they feel is intelligent. A pet animal might fit the description or you might want to take a trip to the zoo to be able to study and draw the animals.

2. Have the children draw the live animal from several angles. Much more will be learned about this "smart" animal by drawing a live creature, rather than drawing a picture from a photograph.

3. At the bottom of the page, have the children list the reasons why this animal was selected as being intelligent. Can it do tricks? Is it gentle? Does it communicate in some way?

4. Compare drawings and information in the group about the different smart animals.

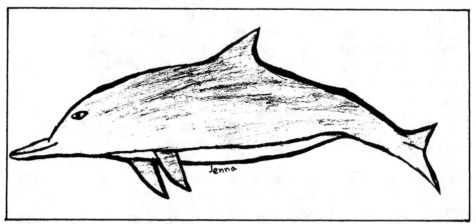

When asked to draw an intelligent animal, this nine-year-old chose to draw a dolphin.

Human dimensions

ONE MUST MARVEL at how humans have adapted as survivors
on the planet. Using our brains, hands, and senses, we have
emerged as a highly adaptable species on earth. Today, more
than five and a half billion of us live in every biome on the
planet. And our numbers continue to grow.

A branch of science called *human ecology* is devoted to the study of
the development and interactions of humans with one another
and their environment. The study of human ecology includes
both a view of early people when humans played an integral but
less destructive role in their ecosystems, and a present-day look
studying the impact humans make upon nature.

No ecosystem left on earth is undisturbed by the effects of
human actions. Our growing population has made a costly
impact on the earth. In many locations, nature has been
depleted. In order to have water, food, shelter, and maintain
enough space to live, we have influenced the course of rivers,
the soil's composition, the plants that grow on the hillsides, and
the animals that remain in the wild. We have used nature to our
advantage for so long that we have come to perceive ourselves
as in control of nature, but in fact, we are thoroughly dependent
on it. We depend on the plants' ability to photosynthesize and
transfer the energy from the sun. We rely on a food chain that
depends on tiny microbes being able to sustain themselves. We
depend on a diversity of plant and animal species to ensure that
our future food and health needs are met. Indeed, people are
interrelated with all elements of the earth.

This chapter introduces human ecology by offering
investigations and activities to help children understand some
adaptations that have helped in our survival; they will study
their hands, senses, and imaginations. To better understand
how people have generated ideas and communicated them,
activities explore use of murals, story telling, nature writing,
keeping a sketchbook/journal, and photographing nature. The
chapter concludes with activities that investigate how we have
made waste into a dangerous rather than natural component of

115

nature, and also how a child can find a special place of one's own, including thoughts on how to preserve it.

By understanding how our bodies work, our history on the earth, and how we perceive the natural world, we can better understand ourselves and our connections with nature. We can continue to use our hands, senses, and brains and learn to live more lightly on the earth. Exploring nature through science and art will enable your children to better understand their own relationship to one another and to the natural world.

1. Why is the human hand so miraculous?

Each human hand includes a framework of 27 bones, giving the hand its shape and form. *Bones* make the hand strong, yet delicate enough to perform many challenges. Along with the bones are about 30 hand muscles. *Muscles* are lengths of tissue. Hand muscles make it possible to move the fingers and thumb. Human thumbs can be moved so they are opposite the other fingers. That is why they are called *opposable thumbs*. An opposable thumb lets you grasp objects and hold them. Monkeys and apes also have opposable thumbs.

Holding and grasping allows hands to perform all kinds of amazing tasks, from shooting a basketball to picking up a contact lens. Throughout time, people have used their hands to manipulate tools, such as plows and saws, thereby influencing their environment. Human hands have helped to mold the appearance of much of nature today.

Our hands help us use tools and perform many tasks.

116   Human dimensions

Information to read aloud and research with your children:

A fun investigation to demonstrate the importance of your thumbs is done by taping them with masking tape to the palms of your hand. Now, try to do simple daily tasks, like buttoning a shirt, tying your shoe laces, or drinking a glass of water with one hand. What other tasks do you find challenging? Imagine how different history would have been if people had not had thumbs and the ability to use tools.

Research and discover why most people are right-handed and fewer are left-handed. You can tell which hand a person favors, even with your eyes closed! Close your eyes and have the person draw the profile of a face. Open your eyes, retrieve the drawing, and predict their handedness by understanding that people who are right-handed usually draw the profile facing the left. Left-handed people usually draw it facing the right. Can you think of other tests to demonstrate handedness? Do you know anyone who is ambidextrous?

Indoor or outdoor activity
Time needed: Open
Materials needed:

Drawing your own hand

- ❑ Sketchbook/journal or drawing paper
- ❑ Pencils
- ❑ Drawing boards

1. Drawing one's own hand is a challenge that many have never tried. The object of this drawing is to study the structure of the human hand while learning what it is possible of accomplishing. Instruct the children to draw the hand that is used the least. If right-handed, draw the left hand, and vice versa.

2. Prepare to draw by having the children work independently, to enable individuals to concentrate.

3. Each child should place their hand to be drawn in a comfortable position just above the drawing paper. Mark the hand's placement by loosely tracing its position on a piece of paper so it can be repositioned if the hand is moved.

1. Why is the human hand so miraculous?   117

4. Using the pencils and paper, encourage the children to work quietly to be able to notice and include every wrinkle, curve, and bump that occurs on the hand. Allow as much time to work as needed.

5. After the children have finished, ask them if they noticed anything new in their hands during their drawing. Because this activity encouraged realistic drawing, there may be some who felt more proud and others who felt more disappointed in their drawing. Let the children know that drawing "realistic" can be very challenging and usually gets easier after practice. Encourage them to keep drawing!

2. How important is our sense of smell?

Our sense of smell keeps us healthy and happy in many ways. The human nose warms up air before it goes to the lungs, keeps out dust and bacteria, and sends odors to the olfactory bulb high up inside the nose. The bulbs have cells with very tiny "hairs." Odors trigger these hairs to send messages to the brain. These messages to the brain can result in automatic responses from the nervous system. For example, pleasant food odors may stimulate the production of saliva or gastric juices in the digestive system. Foul odors can cause gagging or even vomiting. A sense of smell can even save lives by warning of dangers such as smoke or poisonous gases. And it can help taste buds to warn a person not

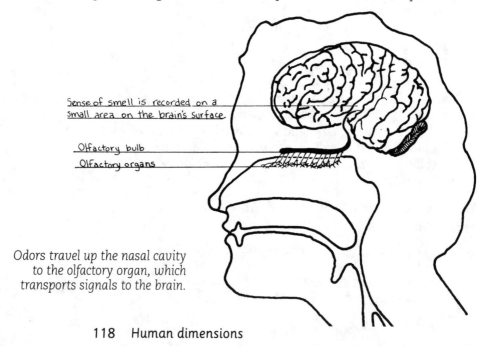

Sense of smell is recorded on a small area on the brain's surface

Olfactory bulb

Olfactory organs

Odors travel up the nasal cavity to the olfactory organ, which transports signals to the brain.

118   Human dimensions

to consume spoiled foods or toxic liquids. Many smells can trigger memories from long ago. The sense of smell is said to trigger memory better than any of the other senses. Can you remember the smell of a favorite relative's house? Often, we don't know if we remember an odor or not until we smell it again!

An odor is made up of tiny particles that are breathed in with the air. The kind of odor depends on the shape of the particle. Have you noticed that when you walk into a bakery or a beauty shop you notice a very distinct odor or aroma? But, after a few minutes you are hardly aware of the odor any longer? Apparently, our sense of smell gets tired easily, so we "get used to" certain odors relatively fast.

Information to read aloud and research with your children:

Research questions

The earliest sense of smell developed millions of years ago in very primitive forms of life. Even though our sense of smell is very helpful, compared to many other animals' smelling abilities, ours is weak. For example, some insects can locate mates many miles away by smell alone. Do some library research and compare our sense of smell to a dog's or a bear's sense of smell. Can you think of an investigation to test a dog's sense of smell versus a human's?

Does your nose help you remember things? Try a blindfolded investigation and see if your nose helped you to be able to identify things. Do some people have a better ability to smell things than others? Can you create an investigation to try to prove this?

Drawing scents from nature

Indoor or outdoor activity
Time needed: 30 minutes, after you collect supplies
Materials needed:

- ❑ Sketchbook/journal
- ❑ Pencils
- ❑ Baby-food jars
- ❑ White paper
- ❑ Tape
- ❑ Scissors
- ❑ Pleasant odorous objects from nature such as orange slices, pine needles, herbs, honeysuckle, cut grass, moist soil, rose petals, clover, cut apples, wood shavings, pond water, seaweed

2. How important is our sense of smell?   119

1. Have the children help you collect various objects from nature and enclose them individually in the baby jars. Cut pieces of white paper and tape them around the jars to conceal the contents of the jars. You, alone, should then number each jar, beginning with #1.

2. Sit in a circle, with the sketchbook/journals and drawing tools on the floor behind each child. Arrange the closed, numbered jars in the center of the circle. Walk with the #1 jar around the circle and let each child sniff it by opening it while they keep their eyes closed.

3. After sniffing, the children are not to announce what it was they smelled, but rather, turn around and draw what was in the jar. When they are done drawing they can turn back into the circle, but they are not to discuss with the other children what they believed the object was, until all of the jars have been smelled.

4. When everybody is turned back into the circle, take the number #2 jar around. Continue until all the jars have been sniffed. Tell the group that if they didn't smell anything, draw a big question mark next to the number.

5. After all the jars have been smelled, discuss and compare the drawings to see if most of them agreed. Then, go through the jars and let them know the order of the contents. Empty out the jars promptly, or the odors won't be so pleasant!

3. How do our ears work?

Our ears actually consist of three divisions: the outer ear, the middle ear, and the inner ear. The outer ear's main function is to catch sounds. Many animals have outer ears that actually rotate and lift up, to catch as much sound as possible. While our ears do not raise up, we often turn our heads in the direction of a sound and will often cup our hands around our ears to try to capture more sound vibrations. These trapped vibrations are then sent down the auditory canal to the eardrum. The *eardrum* is a membrane that vibrates when the sound waves strike it.

Behind the eardrum is the *middle ear*. This area is hollow except for three small connected bones. They are called the *hammer*, *anvil*, and *stirrup*. They are connected to each other as well as

the eardrum and the rear wall of the middle ear. When the eardrum vibrates, these bones are set in motion. This motion is carried into the inner ear. Within this final compartment is the *cochlea*, a snail-like compartment filled with liquid and the ends of hearing nerves. These nerve endings send the vibrations through the auditory nerve and to the front part of the brain, called the *cerebrum*. The cerebrum is the hearing center of the brain. The message is received and the sounds are recognized.

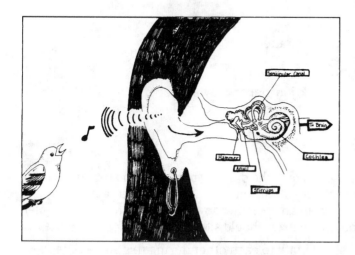

The outer ear captures sound and sends it to the middle ear, which sends it to the brain.

Ears are not only organs of hearing but also organs of balance. Ears help people stay upright. When you spin around very fast, you feel dizzy for a few moments afterward because the fluid in the canals is still moving. Receptor cells are situated in and near the semicircular canals. As you bend or lean, tiny calcium crystals roll over the receptor cells. They report to your brain about your position in relation to the pull of gravity. Even if you swim under water with your eyes shut, your ears will help tell you which direction is up!

Information to read aloud and research with your children:

Research questions

Nature's sounds often create emotional responses in people. The crunching of fall leaves beneath your feet, the sound of waves lapping onto a beach, or the songs of birds in summer

are just some of the sounds of nature that can trigger feelings in people. What sounds in nature do you especially enjoy? Are there nature sounds that scare you or make you feel uncomfortable? For example, many people fear thunder's crashing sound during storms. Do you know how this sound is made? Research and figure out how the nature sounds that you fear are made. Often, once you understand a sound, it no longer will make you feel as afraid.

Drawing the sounds of nature

Outdoor activity
Time needed: 30 minutes
Materials needed:

- ❑ Sketchbook/journal or drawing paper
- ❑ Large variety of crayons, colored pencils, markers, or paints
- ❑ Drawing boards

1. Have the group take the drawing materials and set out for a walk into nature. While on the nature hike, perhaps in a wooded area, in an open meadow, or along a creek, find a quiet spot and each person should sit quietly alone for 15 minutes.

2. No one should talk to each other during this alone time. Begin by relaxing and listening to the surrounding sounds. Prepare to draw.

3. Everyone should draw at least five different nature sounds that they hear during their "alone time" experience. Illustrate the sounds by doing three steps for each sound. First, very quietly, try to make the nature sound. Second, choose a color that seems to fit the sound. Finally, make an abstract mark on the paper to signify the sound. Encourage the children not to debate or think too long about their mark, but to move quickly and let themselves be surprised with the outcome. For example, they needn't draw a bird if they hear a bird song, but a symbol of what that bird song sounded like to them.

4. This activity allows the children to understand that abstract images can be inspired from nature's sounds and inner feelings. It helps them to realize that listening to nature can conjure up moods, colors, and images.

Some of the earliest and most famous examples of early mural art are found in Europe. The caves at Lascaux, France, are the best known of the many prehistoric sites. The Lascaux caves were discovered by accident in 1940 by some boys whose dog had fallen into a hole; that hole led to a chamber of primitive art work. The images at Lascaux are of animals that were hunted: bison, deer, horses, and cattle. The animals are portrayed naturalistically from a side view and appear racing across the walls and ceilings in wild profusion, some only in a black outline and others filled in with bright earth colors. All of the animal images were found deep within the cave, hidden away from the elements and intruders.

The people who made these murals are called the *Magdalenians*. The art is believed to be linked with certain hunting rituals. Two theories speculate as to why the Magdalenians made pictures to accompany their hunting. People believe it was either a ritual that would ensure a successful kill or it was meant to magically attract more animals in their area. Depicted with the animals are also spears and traps, showing how these people hunted.

Archaeologists date the cave paintings by a process called *radiocarbon dating*. According to this method, the art found in Lascaux is believed to be from 15,000–13,000 B.C.

Information to read aloud and research with your children:

Research questions

Early people often made pictures to communicate their thoughts because they didn't have a written language. But they did communicate by using pictures. Does it make sense to you when people say that art and music are international languages? How is art an international language?

In what ways is a picture done by a group of people different than one done by an individual? Would you prefer to take part in drawing a group mural or would you rather do a picture by yourself? Why? If a group of your friends were going to design a large nature mural and paint it, what would your mural be about? What message about nature would you like to illustrate to others?

Drawing a group mural

Indoor or outdoor activity
Time needed: 30 minutes–1 hour (to design the mural on paper with markers and crayons—longer to paint on a fence or wall)
Materials needed:

- ❏ Large sheets of butcher paper (approximately 7×3 feet)
- ❏ Felt-tip markers
- ❏ Crayons
- ❏ Flat surface for drawing

1. Discuss memories of a recent nature outing. Have the group make a plan for a mural that would capture the physical features and the feeling of what the trip included.

A group mural gets the whole group talking, planning, and drawing.

2. Divide the group so that there are no more than eight children per mural, or increase the size of the paper.

3. Use many colors, patterns, and images that help to unify the mural so that it has the feeling of a cohesive project.

4. Present and display the murals so the whole group and their friends can enjoy them.

5. Discuss the possibility of doing another mural on a school wall or a construction fence. This mural could have a theme to educate and attract attention about a threatened local environment that concerns your group. Examples of ideas could include: the need to protect natural habitat by controlling development, the need for more tree planting to protect air quality, or the need to protect local watersheds by not allowing any toxics or oil to be dumped in storm sewers. Your mural will demonstrate how drawings can serve to communicate important ideas.

5. What were some of the first tools?

Early people made tools by sharpening shells, bones, and rocks they found close to their homes. *Flint* and *obsidian* were two rocks that were used for arrowheads and spear points. Flint is a hard quartz that sparks when struck with steel. Obsidian is an acid-resistant, lustrous, volcanic, glass-like rock that can be shaped and broken to a very fine edge, as sharp as glass, that makes a fine cutting tool. Obsidian originates from the most rapid cooling of lava, leaving the mineral black, shiny and smooth.

Arrowheads made from obsidian or flint were flaked from a core rock by hitting it with a larger stone, called a *hammerstone*. The flake was then chipped with an antler tool, from a deer. The material for the arrowhead was grasped in the palm of the hand; a leather pad protected the hand from being cut by the sharp flakes. The flaking by the antler tool was laborious, a skill that often the elderly men knew much better than the young boys. Women rarely made arrowheads.

Arrowhead points were attached directly to the end of the arrow by *sinew* (a tendon) lashings and sticky pitch (from the trees). The arrows were made usually from either willows or alders. As these early cultures evolved, people traded their resources for distant tools that were even better for cutting, spearing, and hunting prey.

Research questions   *Information to read aloud and research with your children:*

Research and get to know more about the early Native Americans that lived in your region. Explore how they made some of their early tools. Often people had to trade for knives and metals. With whom did the Native Americans of your area trade with for other tools?

What are some of the tools that we use regularly? Scissors, razor blades, and ultra-sharp knives are cutting tools that have replaced sharpened shells, rocks, and bones. Imagine how convenient a pair of scissors would appear to a person who only had sharp rocks to use for trying to cut materials! What are some other tools you use? Do you know how to use the tools that are kept in a carpenter's toolbox? Do you feel comfortable using a hammer, screwdriver, wrench, and pliers? Research and construct a pulley, lever, and balance. These are all important tools.

Stencil drawings   Indoor or outdoor activity
Time needed: 30 minutes
Materials needed:

- ❑ Craft knife or scissors
- ❑ Pencils
- ❑ Paper
- ❑ Tempera paint
- ❑ Paintbrush
- ❑ Watercolor paper

1. After talking about tools, do this stencil activity. Discuss with the children how the materials used in this activity are tools. Stress safety if the children are using craft knives, as they are razor sharp!

2. Each child should draw nature designs that will make a good stencil; for example, shapes of a flower, a pine tree, or a butterfly. Draw the nature shape on paper. Cut the shape out with scissors or a craft knife.

3. Next, trace the cutout shape on the thick paper, such as watercolor paper. The thick paper will become the stencil.

126   *Human dimensions*

Lift off the cutout shape and cut the thick paper very carefully to form the stencil.

4. To print, tape the stencil to the surface that will be printed, such as a large sheet of butcher paper.

5. The tempera paint should be mixed to a thick consistency. Brush it over the entire stencil. Do not lift up the stencil until it is completely dry. Then, lift it gently off the paper.

6. The stencil may be used over and over, using the same or other colors. Often stencils are used to make a repeating pattern. Use the stencils to make environmental posters or to decorate a room. Talk about how the tools helped make the stencil and how the stencil is a tool itself.

Making stencils develops the children's skills in drawing, cutting, and painting.

Many early Native Americans used sinew—ligaments that attach muscle to bone—for a version of thread and needles made of bone. They would use these sewing tools when they were attaching animal skins together to make blankets, moccasins, and winter clothes. The leather would be poked with a sharp tool, such as a deer antler, to form a hole that the sinew could be pulled through. Many of the blankets for men

6. What did early Native Americans use for sewing & weaving?

and women were made from the skins of various animals, such as the deer, bear, mountain lion, buffalo, and coyote.

In the Southwest, many people were weavers and spinners. They raised sheep, spun wool, and wove fabric. This fabric was then sewn to make clothes, rugs, and blankets.

West Coast Indians used a *tule* grass, or small bulrush, that they broke off from the stalks with sharp flints or their fingernails. They then bleached, and wove them into breechcloths. Milkweed was used to make string, cord, and nets. The inner bark was dried, then crushed by the Indians' teeth. Sometimes the bark was stripped and the milkweed core was twisted into strands of very fine thread. The most common blanket for the West Coast Indians were those made by winding narrow strips of rabbit skin around milkweed cords to form a loose but warm cover. Indian hemp was also used to make nets, string, and cord. The people would gather this stalk-like plant and roll and twist the fibers into a strong string.

Research questions

Information to read aloud and research with your children:

Sewing has come a long way since people used bones and sinew to attach skins together. Technology has created sewing machines and fabrics that have changed the way we dress and the way we think of sewing. Today we have fabrics that are fireproof, waterproof, and cloth of many textures and colors. Can you think of another innovation in sewing and fabrics that would improve them? How do you think people will sew and use fabrics in the future? What technology will be needed to bring about the changes you imagine?

Drawing and sewing a fabric wall hanging

Indoor or outdoor activity
Time needed: Several hours
Materials needed:

❑ Paper
❑ Pencils
❑ Needles
❑ Thread
❑ 8-x-8-inch squares of fabric

❏ Scissors
❏ Cloth scraps (felt works great)

1. This is a group activity; each person will design a square or several squares to compose a fabric wall hanging.

2. The design of the squares should be based on a group outdoor experience, whether it was to the mountains, zoo, local park, or pond.

3. First, each person can draw a design for their square on a sheet of paper. Then, cut the paper into a pattern and trace the shapes onto the fabric scraps. Make sure that everyone cuts out the shapes and carefully arranges them on the square before beginning to sew.

4. Allow the children to stitch the square using any color of thread they want. Some squares can have the pieces stuffed with cotton for added relief.

5. Finally, sew the squares onto a solid color background, with each square being placed several inches from the others.

6. Hang the finished wall hanging on display for all the children to see. Discuss how the wall hanging reminds them of the trip that it was based on. Also, have the children consider and contrast how people sew today compared to the early ways of Native Americans.

The history of sewing and fabrics can be discussed while doing a group wall hanging.

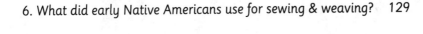

6. What did early Native Americans use for sewing & weaving?   129

7. Why do people tell stories?

The ability to communicate with language is something that we grow up learning how to do. By the time a child is a few years old, most are beginning to tell stories using language. By speaking, we can describe tales with beautiful details, share exciting events, and teach one another things. Storytelling can help give directions, encourage listening skills, and share information. Language helps us solve problems and activate imaginations.

Telling stories is magical because it can transport listeners to other worlds. Stories can pass on beliefs, traditions, and history to others. Stories are easier to remember, and more fun to listen to, than the stating of facts. Stories can help pass on information, along with the wisdom of life.

Many children enjoy telling stories about nature and stretching their imaginations.

Research questions

Information to read aloud and research with your children:

Does it help to be a good observer to tell stories well?
Can you tell a story to another person? Start with a personal experience, story, or a familiar poem. Another way to practice telling stories is to retell a story that you heard someone else tell. Each time a story is told it will be a little bit different. Each

130   Human dimensions

person puts a little of their own interpretation into the story. After you have practiced telling stories, choose one from the library that reflects something in nature that interests you. Can you find stories about animals, trees, flowers, or the earth that you would want to tell?

Indoor or outdoor activity
Time needed: 30 minutes to 1 hour
Materials needed:

- ❏ Sketchbook/journal or drawing paper
- ❏ Colored pencils or markers
- ❏ Knowledge of stories or books to read

1. Read or tell a story related to nature. All children enjoy having stories told to them. The recommended reading list starting on page 147 is just a sampling of some of the good books and stories available.

2. If you are reading a book, don't show the cover or the illustrations of the book. You want the characters to appear in the children's imaginations without the aid of pictures.

3. Before you begin, let the children know that they are to illustrate two of the characters in the story. Have them refrain from beginning their drawings until after you have finished.

4. After you are finished, encourage the children to ask any questions they want about the story. Let them know that they are to draw any scene of the story, but they should include two of the main characters in their illustration. Have the children work independently, relying on their own imaginations.

5. After the children are finished, have them look at the other drawings and see how the main characters appeared according to everyone else. Lead a discussion where you emphasize that all of the illustrations are accurate, and that there is no right or wrong way for a character to appear as they came from each child's imagination.

6. Explain that when the children read books without illustrations, their imaginations get to have more fun creating the images. The more they learn to tell stories and develop the ability to listen to stories, the more vivid the children's imaginations will be.

7. Why do people tell stories?   131

8. Why did John Muir keep a sketchbook/journal?

John Muir (1838–1914) was a naturalist, poet, geologist, farmer, conservationist, writer, botanist, and philosopher. His life's work was to understand and experience nature as thoroughly as he could and to foster that appreciation in others. Because of his efforts, millions of acres of land were preserved. Muir is an example of illustrating how one person can make a difference in helping to preserve nature.

Muir kept sketchbook/journals for several reasons. First of all, sketchbook/journals allowed him to illustrate the rocks, plants, and animals he saw. People didn't have portable cameras in his day, and small sketches provided visual memories of the life and land he saw. Sketchbook/journals were also used to record thoughts and ideas he considered soon after crawling on rocks behind waterfalls, climbing to the peaks of granite mountains, or walking along rivers.

Muir used these journals to refer back to when writing magazine articles, books, and letters. Because of his writing efforts, people of today have become more interested in nature, conservation, and adventure in the out-of-doors. He also became well-known and respected through his writings.

Finally, Muir's sketchbook/journals have become very valuable in the historical sense. They are carefully written illustrated records of the natural environment of his time. Muir took the time to record his thoughts and expressions, helping to chronicle his adventures. If he hadn't written down his thoughts, they would have been lost forever, and we wouldn't know as much about this inspiring man and the land as we do.

Research questions

Information to read aloud and research with your children:

Had you ever heard of John Muir before? He was an early *naturalist*, or someone who studies nature and is interested in all of its aspects. Today, many naturalists are working to help preserve nature. Some are scientists, others are teachers, artists, writers, or photographers. All kinds of people can be naturalists. Do you consider yourself a naturalist? Can you name some other people who are naturalists? A sketchbook/journal can be a great tool for recording your memories and improving your writing and drawing skills. Have you ever kept a sketchbook/journal before? What sort of places would you take a sketchbook/journal with you these days?

Drawing and writing in a sketchbook/journal can develop into a lifelong habit.

Making a sketchbook/journal

Indoor or outdoor activity
Time needed: 30 minutes–1 hour
Materials needed:

- ❑ Spiral-bound drawing book
- ❑ Fabric of child's choice
- ❑ Clear acetate paper
- ❑ Scissors
- ❑ Glue
- ❑ Pressed flowers or favorite drawing

1. The following instructions are suggestions on how children can make their sketchbook/journal. First, cut a piece of fabric to cover the front and back cover of the sketchbook/journal. Glue the fabric down carefully.

2. On the inside front flap, arrange either pressed flowers or a favorite drawing and glue them down. A favorite quotation or saying also helps to personalize it.

3. Cover both the fabric and the inside flaps with clear contact paper. This will adhere the surfaces as well as protect the book from moisture.

4. The aim of this activity is for the child to make such a special sketchbook/journal that he or she will enjoy writing, drawing, and recording nature in it.

9. Why do people write about nature?

Nature is a common thread in all of our lives. Yet, even though we live surrounded by nature, we often stay within our houses and schools, and miss many of the moments that occur in the natural world. Books can take us into those moments, and many authors know how to capture our attention. Through books, we can read and imagine wild animals resting in their dens, hunting at night, and raising their young. Nature books can inspire us to travel to distant places with descriptions of snowshoe walks through the woods or rafting white water rapids. Nature provides an exciting backdrop in adventure stories that may include floods, hurricanes, volcanoes, or earthquakes.

When we read books that vividly portray nature, we learn more about the natural world and ourselves. We learn what inspires us and what we hope to experience for ourselves someday. We can also learn information about how the natural world works. We can learn that the many processes of nature, such as the energy flow from the sun, nature cycles, and adaptations not only apply to plants and animals but also apply to ourselves as well.

Reading books about nature to your children can inspire and excite their imaginations.

If you are going to write and illustrate a nature book, which do you attempt to do first, write the text or draw the pictures? How many words do you want on each page? Look through many books before you begin to write your own nature book and notice how these books are arranged. Try to limit your book to one topic that interests you or that you know a great deal about. What topic would that be for you? What research would you need to do to prepare for writing and illustrating your own nature book?

Indoor activity
Time needed: Several hours
Materials needed:

Writing and illustrating a nature book

- ❏ Nature books for ideas and inspiration
- ❏ Scissors
- ❏ Glue
- ❏ Stapler
- ❏ Drawing paper
- ❏ Cover-stock paper
- ❏ Colored pencils or markers

1. Each individual should spend time researching and writing their nature-oriented story before making the physical structure of the book.

2. As their story is developing, encourage the children to make little *thumbnail sketches* for illustration ideas. Thumbnail sketches are tiny little sketches that shouldn't take more than a minute. These are used to plan out future picture ideas.

3. Once a story is well organized on scratch paper and the little sketches are formulated, have the children decide how many pages the book will require. Fold pieces of drawing paper in half, in order that each piece will provide four pages for the book. For example, if the book will require 12 pages, you'll need three pieces of drawing paper.

4. Have the children write and draw the story on the paper before stapling the pages together. Then any pages that get spilled on or that the children feel don't look "right" can be redone without tearing the book apart. They can use a

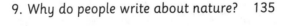

computer for printing the words and then cut and paste them, or use neat handwriting. Other illustration options besides drawing would be to use pictures from a magazine or personal photos.

5. Save the cover for last and have it include the title, author's name, and a vivid illustration that captures the story.

6. Staple the project together. If the book has so many pages that a stapler won't work, staple sections of three pages together at a time, then have the child stitch the entire book together with a needle and thread.

7. Assemble all the nature books and have the children take turns reading them aloud and showing the pictures to the group.

10. Why is hazardous waste a human concept?

Everything in nature is recycled. That is, everything is always becoming something else. When a tree dies, it decomposes with the help of fungi, insects, and weather, and becomes soil in which new growth will occur. Animal waste, or *scat*, is not thought of as hazardous in an animal's habitat. Their scat returns to the soil, enriching it in return. Humans are the only terrestrial animals who put their waste in water. We defecate into toilets, which use water as an effective method of transportation to carry the waste matter to either treatment plants or into our oceans or lakes. We believe that by flushing it away, it goes to a safe place. In many cases, water sources have become contaminated by sewer systems that do not work properly. In this situation, human waste becomes a hazardous waste.

Recycling stations are becoming more popular around the country. It is now possible in most cities and towns to return used newspaper, glass, and metal to recycling centers. Many cities have areas to take plant cuttings after yard work is finished. Organic matter from households is being deposited in backyard compost piles and is being used in gardens in many areas. Products such as oil from cars and CFCs from air conditioners and refrigerators can be recycled in specialized recycling centers. Certain toxins such as medicines, house-cleaning poisons, and batteries are examples of hazardous waste that should not be deposited without taking it to a hazardous waste disposal site. If your city or town is not equipped with the recycling centers needed to handle all your area's waste products, help develop one.

Making a sculpture out of recyclables can educate others about what can be taken to their local recycling center.

Information to read aloud and research with your children:

Research questions

Have you wondered how a landfill works? Try an investigation where you gather together everything that you would normally throw away after lunch. Take this material and dig a hole and bury the lunch debris. Mark the area with a large rock or stake. After two months, dig up the remains of the lunch leftovers and see what you have discovered. If you only threw away food products, such as banana peels, these organic materials will decompose rapidly. But if you also threw away milk cartons,

10. Why is hazardous waste a human concept?   137

aluminum foil, and plastic sandwich bags, they will not decompose for a long time. Imagine how much garbage is generated everyday from your school cafeteria. Is your school recycling materials? Help organize a recycling center and a garden with a compost pile.

Litter sculpture

Indoor or outdoor activity
Time needed: 1 hour
Materials needed:

- ❑ Found litter (not to be taken from trash cans)
- ❑ Gloves
- ❑ Glue
- ❑ String
- ❑ Tacks
- ❑ Scissors

1. To show how litter can be recycled to form art, have the children wear gloves and go out with large plastic bags to pick up trash in an area that is noted for being a mess. Have them dump their found objects and examine them. Make sure they notice the texture in carpet scraps, the shine of aluminum cans, or the labels on wooden fruit crates.

2. This activity works well with children working in small groups. Each sculpture should be at least 2 feet high. Assemble the sculptures using string, glue, tacks, and scissors.

3. Arrange to display the sculptures where many people can view them, for example a school, shopping center, or town center. The sculptures will display how the children are concerned about trash being dumped in their area.

11. How can photography help to communicate about nature?

Photography is a form of communication and good photographs should have something to say. A scene or subject must be interesting to the photographer, in order to inspire interest in anyone else. Cameras, lenses, tripods, and so forth are tools. Although they are important, the picture you take should start in your surroundings and in your head, and the tools will help to capture it. An inexpensive camera can take wonderful pictures if the photographer does more than randomly point and click. To make good pictures, you must be selective about subject matter, try to compose the scene in the viewfinder, and consider the light source.

138 *Human dimensions*

Taking photographs can help to communicate about nature.

Most of us who take pictures enjoy showing them to others. In this way, photographs help others understand a place we have come to know. Photographs can be used to capture beautiful places in nature we enjoy, or they can be used to capture polluted areas that bother us. Photographs can be used to illustrate the different seasons. We can take pictures of our friends and family enjoying aspects of nature. Still-life photographs of sea shells, pine cones, or rocks can illustrate the beautiful shapes and colors found in nature. In short, we can use photographs to communicate to others about the natural world we have come to know, and to remind ourselves of the places we have been.

Information to read aloud and research with your children:

Research questions

Have you ever wondered how cameras work? Do research and compare how a camera and the human eye are similar. Can you make a simple box camera? Research and explore the history of photography. How has photography influenced science and art?

You can take "human-camera" pictures when you don't have your camera with you. When you see something beautiful or something

you especially want to remember in nature, take a "human-camera" picture. First, stare silently at the scene. Then, close your eyes for a few seconds and visualize the scene. Then, open your eyes just for two seconds to capture it, and, quickly, close them again. The concentration and visualization of the image will help keep the scene with you to draw or recall from later.

Photograph walk and drawings

Outdoor activity
Time needed: 1 hour for the walk; another for the drawings
Materials needed:

- ❑ Cameras
- ❑ Color film
- ❑ Drawing paper
- ❑ Pencils
- ❑ Erasers
- ❑ Colored pencils

1. Before you leave on a nature walk, discuss the reasons for taking pictures. Good reasons include to record places and memories, and to communicate about those places.

2. Each child should plan to take pictures of nature during your walk. Later, after the pictures have been developed, the child should select one of the pictures to draw.

3. Encourage the group to be careful in the shooting of the pictures. Keep the light source behind the camera as much as possible. Take plenty of time in composing the pictures in the viewfinders. Encourage the children to get as close to their subject matter as possible. Remind them that they are shooting pictures that they will attempt to draw later. By having only one roll of film, the children are limited in the number of shots they can take. Remind them to use their film with careful consideration.

4. Once the pictures have been developed, have the children select one picture they wish to draw. They should sketch the image first on the drawing paper. After they are satisfied with the sketch, encourage them to color in their drawing with their colored pencils.

5. Hang the photos next to the finished drawings and have each child describe where they took the picture and why it was something they wanted to photograph and draw.

While taking a walk in the woods or along a river, certain places capture our attention where we spend time observing or feeling reflective. What is it that draws people to these special places? While some people are compelled to climb and take in the grand view from the top of a mountain or canyon, others might prefer to sit along a slow meandering stream below. Others might choose to climb to the top of a tree or behind a large boulder in order to be alone and hidden from others. Many special places need not be dramatic; they may be found in one's own backyard, the local city park, or on the school grounds.

Spending time in these special places can be a means for observing and learning more about nature. Do not mark or change your place, leave it just as you found it. Once you have found your own special place, you should try to return there again and again. Note how the area changes with the seasons and look closely how other animals and elements of nature are interacting with the same area.

Information to read aloud and research with your children:

Have you ever had a special place before? Do you still have one? What elements of nature made it special for you? Find one for yourself and try to spend some time there once a week. What sorts of changes would you notice over the course of a year? Did you ever have a special place that was destroyed by road or building construction? How did that make you feel? What besides the special place often gets destroyed during construction activities? Why is it important to keep some places safe from development?

Indoor and outdoor activity
Time needed: Will vary to group
Materials needed:

- ❑ Several maps to show for examples
- ❑ Sketchbook/journal or drawing paper
- ❑ Pencils

12. Why do some places capture our attention?

Research questions

Drawing a map to your special place

1. Discuss the parts of a map while showing examples of maps. Include information about scales, legends, and landmarks. Talk about how the tops of maps always face north and the consistency of the other directions.

2. After the map talk, each child should find a special place to call their own. Once alone in their special place, they will draw a map of how they got there from memory. Encourage the children to try to determine the different directions, and make the top of their maps face north. Make sure the children include landmarks that stood out to them. Have them mark their special place with an **X**.

Having the opportunity to be away from others and claim a special place can inspire drawing and writing ideas.

3. Once the maps are in a "draft" stage, have each child test their map by retracing their routes back to where everyone began. Have them add any information that would help locate their special place.

4. Next, try to locate another person's special place by using their map. Do this in groups of threes or fours. The person whose place is being discovered should only speak up if the group is having trouble with the map. Once the group finds the individual's special place, have the individual explain why it is special to him or her. Return to the starting place and try another group member's map to their special place.

13. What makes a human community?

A *community* in the biological sense is when organisms are living together in a certain environment and affecting one another in various ways. For example, a forest of trees and undergrowth plants, inhabited by animals and rooted in soil containing bacteria and fungi, constitutes a biological community. Important elements of a community that must be included, and are as vital as the plants and animals, are sunlight, moisture, and air.

Just as there are biological communities found in forests, deserts, grasslands, and mountains, human communities exist throughout the world. A human community can be developed in city neighborhoods. A neighborhood is an area where people often grow to know one another and are willing to work together to improve their living situation. A human community will help to watch out for one another's families, plant gardens and trees, and learn to share common areas. A "community spirit" occurs when people feel a sense of belonging and take responsibility for the people and land that surrounds them.

Information to read aloud and research with your children:

Research questions

How does a biological community differ from a human community? Human communities are made up of people and their interactions, but they are supported by elements of nature. Although many of us move frequently and live in towns or cities where jobs or schools dictate where the family lives, all of our food, clothing, and home building materials originated in nature. Are human communities dependent on nature for their survival?

What are ways that people in your town can develop a positive community spirit? When people feel that they belong to a group they usually feel more secure and want to improve their

surroundings. Do members of your neighborhood play at the same parks? Shop at the same grocery stores or food co-ops? Learn at the same nature center and school? How can you help to develop a positive sense of community through these places?

Building a sustainable community

Outdoor activity
Time needed: 30 minutes
Materials needed:

❑ Sand
❑ Objects from nature

1. Sand piles are accessible near the shores of many streams, lakes, and the ocean. Also, one can often find sand in a schoolyard play area, near construction sites, and in local parks.

2. Once at the sand area, discuss how a healthy human community needs to provide food, water, shelter, sanitation, recreation, and education for it to sustain itself and for its citizens to develop a community spirit.

3. Divide the children into small groups. Each group will design and build in the sand an imaginary community that provides for these needs. Natural resources, such as forests, lakes, or rivers, should be considered. Agricultural areas, residential areas, and wilderness areas should also be included.

4. Little sticks, acorns, rocks, or other found nature objects can be used as props to represent aspects of their community.

5. Have each group explain where their sand environment's water comes from, where the wild places are, and what kind of vegetation grows where. If the children learn to develop their sand communities with environmental planning and sustainability in mind, they will begin to see a need for environmental planning for their own town or city.

Planning a sustainable community is a group effort that requires communication and cooperation.

Additional reading

THE MORE TIME I spend outside, the more I realize how much there is to learn about nature. Nature is an inexhaustible subject, one that can be explored from the termite's habitat to the constellations of the heavens. The best way to become more familiar with this world is to get outside and walk in it, draw it, and explore its ever-changing face, wet and dry, high and low.

John Muir said that "books are but piles of stones set up to show coming travelers where other minds have been." The following bibliography is provided to illustrate supplementary reading material for each chapter. Reading "piles of stones" can prepare you for the outings that you as a parent, teacher, or nature guide are interested in sharing with your children. The following books are a selected few of the many resources available through your public library or bookstore.

Adult reading

Chapter 1: Earth's elements

Beiser, Arthur. *The Earth*. New York: Time-Life Books, 1969.

Dickenson, Terence. *Exploring the Sky by Day*. Camden House Publishers, 1988.

LaChapelle, Dolores. *Earth Wisdom*. Silverton, CO: Fill Hill Arts, 1978.

Lovins, Amory. *Soft Energy Paths*. Cambridge, MA: Ballinger, 1977.

Mason, John. *Power Station Sun: The Story of Energy*. New York: Facts on File, 1987.

Nilsson, Lenhart. *Close to Nature*. New York: Pantheon Books, 1984.

Olson, Sigurd F. *Sigurd F. Olson's Wilderness Days*. New York: Alfred A. Knopf, 1973.

Pringle, Laurence. *Natural Fire, Its Ecology in Forests*. New York: William Morrow & Co., 1979.

Simon, Hilda. *The Magic of Color*. New York: Lothrop, Lee, and Shepard, 1981.

Wallace, David Rains. *The Dark Range—A Naturalist's Night Notebook*. San Francisco, CA: Sierra Club Books, 1978.

Chapter 2: Plant investigations

Andrews, W. A. *A Guide to the Study of Soil Ecology*. Englewood Cliffs, NJ.: Prentice-Hall, Inc., 1973.

Caufield, Catherine. *In the Rainforest*. New York: Alfred A. Knopf, 1985.

Harlow, William M. *Inside Wood, Masterpiece of Nature*. Washington, DC: American Forestry Association, 1970.

Headstrom, Richard. *Surburban Wildflowers: An Introduction to the Common Wildflowers of Your Back Yard and Local Park*. Englewood Cliffs, NJ: Prentice-Hall Press, 1984.

Jackson, James P. *The Pulse of the Forest*. Washington, DC: American Forestry Association, 1980.

Lipkis, Andy and Katie. *The Simple Act of Planting a Tree: Healing Your Neighborhood, Your City, and Your World*. Los Angeles: Jeremy Tarcher, Inc., 1990.

McCormick, Jack. *The Life of the Forest*. New York: McGraw-Hill, Inc., 1966.

Myers, Norman. *The Primary Source, Tropical Forests and Our Future*. New York: W.W. Norton and Co., 1984.

Roth, Charles E. *The Plant Observer's Guidebook*. Englewood Cliffs, NJ.: Prentice-Hall, Inc., 1984.

Stern, Kingsley. *Introductory Plant Biology*. Dubuque, IA: William C. Brown Company Publishers, 1982.

Tilgner, Linda. *Let's Grow: 72 Gardening Adventures with Children*. Pownal, VT: Storey Communications, 1988.

Tomkins, Peter and Christopher Bird. *The Secret Life of Plants*. New York: Harper & Row, 1973.

Walker, Laurence. *Trees: An Introduction to Trees and Forest Ecology for the Amateur Naturalist*. Englewood Cliffs, NJ: Prentice-Hall Press, 1984.

Chapter 3: Animal explorations

Dillard, Annie. *Pilgrim at Tinker Creek*. New York: Bantam Books, 1974.

Grater, Russell K. *Discovering Sierra Mammals*. Yosemite, CA: Yosemite Natural History Association and Sequoia Natural History Association, 1978.

Klots, Alexander B. and Elsie. *1001 Questions Answered About Insects*. New York: Dover Publications, Inc., 1961.

Kohl, Judith and Herbert. *The View from the Oak*. New York: Scribner's, 1977.

Leopold, Aldo. *Sand County Almanac*. New York: Oxford University Press, 1966.

Levine, Sigmund. *Wonders of Animal Disguises*. New York: Dodd, Mead, and Co., 1962.

Morrison, Coldrey and Goldie. *Danger Colors*. New York: Putnam, 1986.

Patent, Dorothy Hinshaw. *How Smart Are Animals?* Orlando, FL: Harcourt Brace Jovanovich, 1990.

Rights, Mollie. *Beastly Neighbors: All About Wild Things in the City*. New York: Little Brown and Co., Yolla Bolly Press, 1981.

Romer, Alfred Sherwood. *Man and the Vertebrates*. Chicago, IL.: University of Chicago Press, 1941.

Storer, Tracy I. and Robert L. Usinger. *General Zoology*. New York: McGraw-Hill Publishers, 1979.

Welty, Joel Carl. *The Life of Birds*. New York: Alfred A. Knopf, 1962.

Chapter 4: Human dimensions

Barrett, Samuel Alfred, and E. W. Gifford. *Miwok Material Culture*. Yosemite, CA: Yosemite Natural History Association, 1933.

Berger, Gilda and Melvin. *The Whole World of Hands*. Boston: Houghton Mifflin, 1982.

Caduto, Michael J. *Keepers of the Earth: Native American Stories and Environmental Activities for Children*. Golden, CO: Fulcrum Press, 1988.

Clarke, James Mitchell. *The Life and Adventures of John Muir*. San Diego, CA: The Word Shop Publisher, 1979.

Hamilton and Weiss. *Children Tell Stories, A Teaching Guide*. Katonah, NY: Richard C. Owen Publishers, 1990.

Kroeber, Theodora. *The Inland Whale*. Berkeley, CA: University of California Press, 1959.

LaPena, Frank and Craig Bates. *Legends of the Yosemite Miwok*. Yosemite, CA: Yosemite Natural History Association, 1981.

McVey, Vicki. *The Sierra Club Wayfinding Book*. New York: Little, Brown and Company, 1989.

Minor, Marz Nono. *American Indian Craft Book*. New York: Popular Library Edition, 1972.

Muir, John. *The Wilderness World of John Muir*. Boston: Houghton Mifflin, 1954.

Neihardt, John. *Black Elk Speaks*. Lincoln, NE: Nebraska Press, 1961.

Storm, Hyemeyohsts. *Seven Arrows*. New York: Ballantine Books, Inc., 1973.

Thoreau, Henry David. *Walden and "Civil Disobedience."* New York: The New American Library of World Literature, 1960.

Weiss, Harvey. *Maps: Getting from Here to There*. Boston: Houghton Mifflin, 1991.

General recommended reading for nature educators

Arnold, Arnold. *The Crowell Book of Arts and Crafts for Children*. New York: T. Y. Crowell Publishers, 1975.

Carlson, Laurie. *Eco Art: Earth Friendly Art and Craft Experiences*. Charlotte, VT: A Williamson Kid's Can! Book, 1993.

Carson, Rachel L. *The Sense of Wonder*. New York: Harper & Row Publishers, 1956.

Cornell, Joseph, Bharat. *Sharing Nature with Children*. Grass Valley, CA: Ananda Publications, 1979.

Franck, Frederick. *The Zen of Seeing: Seeing/Drawing as Meditation*. New York: Vintage Books, Random House, 1973.

Gore, Al. *Earth in the Balance: Ecology and the Human Spirit*. New York: Houghton Mifflin, 1992.

Johnson, Cathy. *Local Wilderness: Observing Neighborhood Nature through an Artist's Eye*. Englewood Cliffs, NJ: Prentice Hall, 1987.

Katz, Adrienne. *Naturewatch: Exploring Nature with Your Children*. London: Addison-Wesley Publishing Co., 1986.

Leslie, Clare Walker. *Nature Drawing: A Tool for Learning*. Englewood Cliffs, NJ: Prentice-Hall, 1980.

Lingelbach, Jenepher. *Hands-On Nature; Information and Activities for Exploring the Environment with Children*. Woodstock, VT: Vermont Institute of Natural Science, 1986.

Nicolaides, Kimon. *The Natural Way to Draw*. Boston: Houghton Mifflin, 1941.

Peppin, Anthea. *Nature in Art*. Brookfield, CT: Millbrook Press, 1991.

Preble, Duane. *We Create Art Creates Us*. New York: Harper & Row, 1976.

Ruess, Everett. *A Vagabond for Beauty*. Layton, UT: Peregrine Smith Books, 1983.

Russel, Helen Ross. *Ten Minute Field Trips*. Washington, DC: National Science Teachers Association, 1973.

Russell, Terry and Renny. *On the Loose*. San Francisco: Sierra Club Books and Ballantine Books, 1967.

Arnosky, Jim. *Near the Sea*. New York: Lothrop, Lee & Shepard, 1990.

Carrighar, Sally. *One Day on Beetle Rock*. Philadelphia: Curtis Publishing Co., 1943.

George, Jean Craighead. *On the Far Side of the Mountain*. New York: E.P. Dutton, 1990.

Giono, Jean. 1985. *The Man Who Planted Trees*. Chelsea, VT: Chelsea Green Publishers, 1985.

Grove, Doris. *A Water Snake's Year*. New York: Macmillan, 1991.

Hiscock, Bruce. *The Big Tree*. New York: Atheneum, 1991.

Nature-oriented books to share with children

Jeffers, Susan. *Brother Eagle, Sister Sky*. New York: Penguin, 1991.

Mayo, Gretchen. *North American Indian Stories*. New York: Walker Publishing Co., 1990.

North, Sterling. *Rascal*. New York: Penguin, 1963.

O'Dell, Scott. *Island of the Blue Dolphins*. Boston: Houghton Mifflin, 1960.

Parnall, Peter. *Quiet*. New York: William Morrow & Co., 1989.

Robertson, Kayo. *Signs Along the River: Learning to Read the Natural Landscape*. Boulder, CO: Roberts Rinehart, 1986.

Ross, Michael. *Cycles, Cycles, Cycles*. Yosemite, CA: Yosemite Natural History Association, 1979.

Rylant, Cynthia. *Every Living Thing*. New York: Aladdin Books, 1988.

Seuss, Dr. *The Lorax*. New York: Random House, 1971.

Taylor, Barbara. *The Animal Atlas*. New York: Random House, 1992.

Nature poetry for children

Bruchac & London. *Thirteen Moons on Turtle's Back: A Native American Year of Moons*. New York: Putnam, 1992.

Dickinson, Emily. *A Brighter Garden*. New York: Philomel, 1990.

Labor, Earle. *Great Works of Jack London*. New York: Harper & Row Publishers, 1970.

Lathem, Edward Connery. *The Poetry of Robert Frost*. New York: Holt, Rinehart and Winston, 1979.

Livingston, Myra. *If the Owl Calls Again: A Collection of Owl Poems*. Mfet K. Elderberry Books, 1990.

Service, Robert. *Best of Robert Service*. New York: Dodd, Mead, and Company, 1953.

Snyder, Gary. *Turtle Island*. New York: New Directions Books, 1974.

Yolen, Jane. *Bird Watch*. New York: Philomel, 1990.

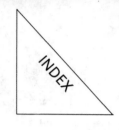

A

absorption, 4
additional reading, 147-152
agriculture, 68
amber, 22
animal explorations, 75-114
  bees and butterflies, 79-81, **79**
  camouflage in animals, 103-106, **104**
  carnivores, 96
  disguises in animals, 106-108, **107**
  earthworms, 83-84, **84**
  feathers, 90-93, **91**
  frog hibernation, 88-90, **89**
  herbivores, 97
  hooves and paws, 96-98, **97**
  intelligence of animals, 113-114, **114**
  light and sound response, 101-103, **102**
  memory of animals, 110-113, **112**
  mollusks, 81-83, **82**
  omnivores, 99
  shelters built by animals, 108-110, **110**
  smallest animals, 76-79, **77**
  spider webs, 85-88, **86**, **87**
  teeth, 98-100
  whiskers on animals, 93-96, **94**, **96**
animal track drawings, 98
annual plants, 47
*anthers, 49
anvil, 120
arrowheads, 125
artistic skills required, xv-xvi

B

balance and ears, 121
barbs, 90
bark on trees, 61-63, **61**
  colors and dyes from bark, 61
  fibers in bark, 61
  fissures, 61
  growth rings in trees, 62
  phloem, 61
  rubbings of bark, 62-63
  sugar in bark, 61
barnacles, 24
bees, xix, 79-81, **79**, 111
biennial plants, 47
biological communities, 143
bioluminescence, 9
brooding patch, 108
butterflies, xix, 79-81

C

camouflage in animals, 103-106, **104**

carbon dioxide, 71
carnivores, 96, 99
carpel, 49
cave paintings, 123-125, **124**
cellulose, 98
charcoal drawing, 33, **33**
chlorophyll, 36, 54
clay soils, 15
clay-making 16-17, **17**
cochlea, 121
collage making, 25-26, **25**
color explorations, 4-7, **4**, **7**
  absorption, 4
  heat absorption of colors, 6
  infrared light, 5
  prisms, 4, 5
  rainbows, 4, 5
  reflection, 4
  spectrum, 4
  sunlight, 4
  warm and cool colors, 6-7, **7**
  watercolor painting, 5-6
  wavelengths, 4
  why we see color, 4-5, **4**
communities of humans, 143-145, **145**
  biological communities, 143
  building a sustainable community, 144
coniferous trees, 56-58, **57**
cycles of nature explorations, 10-12, **11**
  drawing cycles, 11-12
  life cycles, 10
  seasonal cycles, 10
  water cycles, 10

D

dandelions, 51
deciduous trees, 56-58, **57**
decomposition, 32, 59, 137-138
diastrophism, 12-13
disguises in animals, 106-108, **107**
  baby animals in disguise, 107
  camouflage, 106
  hidden animal drawing, 107-108, **107**
  molting, 106
drawing tips, xvi
duff, 58

E

eardrum, 120
ears, 101-103, **102**
  anvil, 120
  balance, 121

cochlea, 121
  drawing sounds of nature, 122
  eardrum, 120
  hammer, 120
  human ears, 120-122, **121**
  middle ear, 120
  nerves and brain, 121
  stirrup, 120
earth's elements, 1-33
  color explorations, 4-7, **4**, **7**
  cycles of nature explorations, 10-12, **11**
  earth-surface changes explorations, 12-14, **14**
  fire ecology, 32-33, **33**
  fossil exploration, 22-24, **22**
  glues in nature exploration, 24-26, **25**
  hurricanes and tornadoes, 28-30
  light explorations, 2-3, **3**
  nighttime explorations, 7-9, **8**
  rock exploration, 20-22, **21**
  sand color exploration, 17-19, **19**
  snow explorations, 30-31, **31**
  soil elements exploration, 15-17, **17**
  wind explorations, 26-28, **28**
earth-surface changes explorations, 12-14, **14**
  diastrophism, 12-13
  earthquakes, 13
  erosion, 12-13
  landscape creation, 13-14, **14**
  sandbars, 13
  temperature of earth, 12
  weathering
earthquakes, 13
earthworms, 83-84, **84**
  aeration of soil, 83
  collecting and observing earthworms, 83-84
  drawing soil creatures, 84, **84**
  reproduction of earthworms, 83
  setae, 83
echolocation in nocturnal animals, 8-9
ecopyrology, 32
erosion, 12-13
eyes, 101-103, **102**

F

feathers, 90-93, **91**
  barbs, 90
  drawing with feathers, 92-93
  follicles, 90
  insulation, 90

feathers, *Continued*
  keratin, 90
  molting, 92
  recognition markings, 92
  rictal bristles, 94
  uses for feathers, 91-92
filaments, 49
fire ecology, 32-33, **33**
  animals in forest fires, 32
  charcoal drawing, 33, **33**
  decomposition by fire, 32
  ecopyrology, 32
  recovering nature after fire, 32-33
  trees depending on fire for seeding, 32
flowers, 49-51, **49**
  anthers, 49
  carpel, 49
  color of flowers, 50
  compound flowers, 50
  filaments, 49
  flower-pattern drawing, 51
  ovary, 49
  parts of flower, 49
  petals, 49
  pollen, 49
  pollination, 50
  scent of flowers, 50
  sepals, 49
  simple flowers, 50
  stamens, 49
  stigmas, 49
follicles, 90
forest succession, 63-65, **64**
  recording types of plants, 63
  transects, succession transects, 64-65, **64**
fossil exploration, 22-24, **22**
  ages of fossils, 22-23
  amber fossils, 22
  clay impressions, 23-24
  formation of fossils, 22
  paleontology, 22
frogs, 88-90, **89**
  hibernation of frogs, 88, 89
  metamorphosis of tadpoles, 89
  potato prints, 89-90
  reproduction, 88
  tadpoles, 88, 89
fruit and seeds explorations, 45-46, **45**
  collecting seeds, 46
  scavenger hunt sketch, 46
  transportation of seeds, 45
fungi, 38

G
glacial polish, 20
glues in nature exploration, 24-26, **25**
  animals that make glue, 24
  barnacles, 24
  collage making, 25-26, **25**
  insects that make glue, 24
  pine pitch, 24

plants that make glue, 24
greenhouse effect, 71

H
hammer, 120
hammerstones, 125
hands, 116-118, **116**
  bones, 116
  drawing your hand, 117-118
  muscles, 116
  opposable thumbs, 116
hazardous wastes, 136-138, **137**
  decomposition, 137-138
  landfills, 137-138
  litter sculptures, 138
  recycling, 136-138, **137**
hearing
  human hearing, 120-122, **121**
heat absorption of colors, 6
herbivores, 97, 98
hermaphrodites, 83
hibernation of animals, 30
hooves and paws, 96-98, 97
human dimensions, 115-145
  communities, 143-145, **145**
  ears and hearing, 120-122, **121**
  hands, 116-118, **116**
  hazardous wastes, 136-138, **137**
  human ecology, 115
  John Muir's sketchbook-journal, 132-134, **133**
  Magdalenian people and cave paintings, 123
  map making, 140-143, **142**
  murals and cave paintings, 123-125, **124**
  photography and nature, 138-140, **139**
  sewing and weaving, 127-129, **129**
  sketchbooks and journals, 132-134, **133**
  smelling and noses, 118-120, **118**
  special places, 140-143, **142**
  storytelling, 130-131, **130**
  tool making, 125-127, **127**
  writing about nature, 134-136, **134**
human ecology, 115
hummingbirds, xix
hurricanes and tornadoes, 28-30
  drawing hurricanes and tornadoes, 29-30
  dust devils, 29
  eye, 28
  speed of wind, 28-29
  twisters, 29
  whirlwinds, 29

I
igneous rocks, 18, 20
infrared light, 5
instinct, 110
intelligence, 110, 113-114, **114**
  drawing a smart animal, 114, **114**

lifespan vs. intelligence, 113
  thinking, 113
invertebrates, 77

J
journals, 132-134, **133**

K
keratin, 90

L
landfills, 137-138
Lascaux cave paintings, 123
lateral lines in fish, 101
leaf litter, 58-61, **59**
  decomposition, 59
  drawing forest floor still life, 60-61
  duff, 58
  insulating properties, 59
  soil formation, 59
leaves, 54-56, **55**
  back-to-back leaf drawings, 55-56, **55**
  chlorophyll, 54
  color changes, 54
  photosynthesis, 54
  structure and shape of leaves, 54-55
lichens, 40-42, **42**
  air quality vs. lichens, 40
  ancient lichens, 40
  animals that eat lichens, 41
  growth rate, 40
  magnifying glass to study lichens, 41-42, **42**
  symbiotic relationships, 40
life cycles, 10
light explorations, 2-3, **3**
  bioluminescence, 2
  light of day drawing, 2-3, **3**
  Milky Way galaxy, 2
  moonlight, 2
  solar system, 2
  starlight, 2
  sunlight, 2
light response in animals, 101-103, **102**
  attracting moths, 102
  drawing night insects, 103
litter sculptures, 138

M
Magdalenian people, 123
magma, 20
map making, 140-143, **142**
mask making, 94-96, **96**
materials and supplies, xvi-xvii
memory of animals, 110-113, **112**
  bee dances, 111
  instinct, 110
  intelligence, 110
  pet memory tests, 111
  testing your memory, 111-113, **112**
metamorphic rocks, 18, 20

metamorphosis, 89
microbes, 76-79, **77**
microscopes, 78-79
middle ear, 120
Milky Way galaxy, 2
mobiles, 27-28, **28**
mollusks, 81-83, **82**
  parts of a mollusk, 81
  snail-and-slug hike drawing, 82-83
  snails and slugs, 81-82
  species of mollusks, 81
molt, 92, 106
moon, 2, 8-9
mosses, 42-44, **43**
  moss-forest drawing, 44
  photosynthesis, 43
  species of mosses, 43
  spores, 43
  ultragreen or luminscent mosses, 43
  water absorption of moss, 43-44
moths, xix
Muir, John, xiv, 132-134
murals and cave paintings, 123-125,
  124
mushrooms, 38-40, **38**
  edible and inedible mushrooms, 39
  fungi, 38
  growing mushrooms, 39
  life cycle of mushrooms, 38
  mycelium, 38
  spore prints, 39-40
  spores, 38
mycelium, 38

N

Native Americans, 127-129
nature areas, xix-xx
nests, 108
nighttime explorations, 7-9, **8**
  bioluminescence, 9
  echolocation in nocturnal animals,
    8-9
  moonlight, 8-9
  nighttime drawings, 8
  nocturnal animals, 8
  starlight, 8
nocturnal animals, 8
noses, 118-120, **118**

O

ocelli in insects, 101
odors, 118-119
olfactory glands, 118
omnivores, 99
ovary of flower, 49
oxygen creation, 37, 68, 71

P

paleontology, 22
paper making, 69-70
paws and hooves, 96-98, **97**
people-helping plants, 68-70
  agriculture, 68

food supplies, 68
medicinal plants, 68
oxygen creation, 68
paper making, 69-70
perennial plants, 47
petals, 49
phloem, 61
photography and nature, 138-140, **139**
photons of light, 36
photosynthesis, 36-38, **36**, 43, 54
  chlorophyll, 36
  leaf patterns, 37
  oxygen creation, 37
  photo paper designs, 37-38
  photons of light, 36
plant investigations, 35-73
  bark on trees, 61-63, **61**
  coniferous vs. deciduous trees, 56-
    58, **57**
  flowers, 49-51, **49**
  forest succession exploration, 63-65,
    64
  fruit and seeds explorations, 45-46,
    45
  leaf litter, 58-61, **59**
  leaves, 54-56, **55**
  lichens, 40-42, **42**
  mosses, 42-44, **43**
  mushrooms, 38-40, **38**
  people-helping plants, 68-70
  photosynthesis, 36-38, **36**
  seed germination, 46-49, **47**
  trees and wildlife, 65-67, **67**
  tropical rain forests, 70-73, **71**
  weeds, 51-53, **53**
poetry for children, 152
pollen, 49
pollination, 50
potato prints, 89-90
pressed flowers, 48-49
prisms, 4, 5
protozoa, 76-77, **77**

R

radiocarbon dating, 123
rain forests, 70-73, **71**
  carbon dioxide absorption, 71
  greenhouse effect, 71
  medicinal plants, 70-71
  migrating birds and rain forests, 71
  oxygen creation, 71
  saving rain forests, 72
  scratch drawing, 72-73
  species in rain forests, 70, 71
rainbows, 4, 5
recognition markings on feathers, 92
recycling, 136-138, **137**
  litter sculptures, 138
red clover, 51
reflection, 4
rictal bristles, 94
rocks, 17-18, 20-22, **21**
  glacial polish, 20

grab bag drawings, 21-22, **21**
igneous, 18, 20
magma, 20
metamorphic rocks, 18, 20
sedimentary, 18, 20
shapes of rock, 20
textures of rock, 20

S

sand color exploration, 17-19, **19**
sandbars, 13
sandy soil, 15
scat, 75
scavenger hunt sketch, 46
scratch drawing, 72-73
seasonal cycles, 10
sedimentary rocks, 18, 20
seed germination (*see also* fruit and
    seeds), 46-49, **47**
  annual species, 47
  biennial species, 47
  perennial species, 47
  planting and germinating seeds, 47,
    47
  pressing plants, 48-49
  seedlings, 47
sepals, 49
setae, 83
sewing and weaving, 127-129, **129**
shelters built by animals, 108-110,
  110
  brooding patch, 108
  dens, 108
  hives, 109
  nests, 108
  snow shelter building, 109-110, **110**
  tunnels and burrows, 108
silt, 15
sketchbooks, 132-134, **133**
skull drawings, 100
smallest animals, 76-79, **77**
  drawing from microscopes, 78-79
  invertebrates, 77
  microbes, 76
  microscopes, 78-79
  protozoa, 76-77, **77**
  sporozoa, 77
  wet mounts for microscopes, 78
smelling (*see also* noses), 118-120, **118**
snow explorations, 30-31, **31**
  forming snow, 30
  hibernation of animals, 30
  insulating property of snow, 30
  measuring snowfall, 31
  sculptures in snow, 31, **31**
  snowfall around the world, 30
  subnivian animals, 30
snow-shelter building, 109-110, **110**
soil elements exploration, 15-17, **17**
  clay, 15
  clay-making , 16-17, **17**
  clay-like soil, 15
  erosion of rocks, 17

soil elements exploration, *Continued*
  igneous rocks, 18
  inorganic material in soil, 15
  living organisms in soil, 15
  metamorphic rocks, 18
  organic material in soil, 15
  sand paintings, 19, **19**
  sandy soil, 15
  sedimentary rocks, 18
  silty soil, 15
  subsoil, 15
  topsoil, 15
solar system, 2
sound response in animals, 101-103,
  102
spectrum of colors, 4
spider webs, 85-88, **86**, **87**
  weaving a web, 87-88, **87**
spores, 38, 39-40, 43
sporozoa, 77
stamens, 49
stars, 2, 8
stigmas, 49
stirrup, 120
storytelling, 130-131, 130
  illustrating your story, 131
subnivian animals, 30
sunlight, 2

sustainable communities, 144
symbiotic relationships, 40

T
tadpoles, 88, 89
teeth, 98-100
  herbivores vs. carnivores, 98-99
  omnivores, 99
  skull drawings, 100
  snakes, 99
thinking, 113
thumbs, opposable thumbs, 116
time requirements for projects, xviii
tool making, 125-127, **127**
  arrowheads, 125
  flint, 125
  hammerstones, 125
  obsidian, 125
  stencil drawings, 126-127, **127**
topsoil, 15
transect, forest-succession transect,
  64-65, **64**
tree hotel drawing, 66, **67**
trees, 56-58, **57**
  bark on trees, 61-63, **61**
  growth rings, 62
  tree hotel drawing, 66, **67**
  wildlife and trees, 65-67, **67**

tropical rain forests (see rain forests)
tympanic organs in insects, 101

W
water cycle, 10
wavelengths of colored light, 4
weathering of rocks, 12-13
weaving a spider web, 87-88, **87**
weaving and sewing, 127-129, **129**
weeds, 51-53, **53**
  dandelions, 51
  growing and drawing weeds, 52-53,
    53
  pollination, 52
  red clover, 51
wet mounts for microscopes, 78
whiskers on animals, 93-96, **94**, **96**
  birds, rictal bristles, 94
  mask making, 94-96, **96**
wind explorations, 26-28, **28**
  direction of winds, 26
  mobiles, 27-28, **28**
  offshore-onshore breezes, 26
  power from wind, 27
  prevailing winds, 26
writing about nature, 134-136,
  134
  illustrating your book, 135-136